WARTIME COURAGE

GORDON BROWN was born in 1951 and went to school in Kirkcaldy and studied at Edinburgh University. From 1976 to 1980 he lectured at Edinburgh University and then Glasgow College of Technology. In May 1983 he became MP for Dunfermline East. He was Opposition spokesperson on Treasury and Economic Affairs (Shadow Chancellor) from 1992. With the election of the Labour government in May 1997, Gordon Brown was made Chancellor of the Exchequer and held the post for ten years. Following the resignation of Tony Blair he became Prime Minister in June 2007. His books include *Maxton*, *The Politics of Nationalism and Devolution*, *Where There is Greed* (co-author), *John Smith: Life and Soul of the Party* (editor), *Speeches 1997–2006*, *Moving Britain Forward* and *Courage: Eight Portraits*. He is married to Sarah Macaulay and they have two sons.

WARTIME COURAGE

Stories of Extraordinary Courage
by Exceptional Men and Women
in World War Two

GORDON BROWN

BLOOMSBURY
LONDON · BERLIN · NEW YORK

First published in Great Britain 2008
This paperback edition published 2009

Bloomsbury Publishing Plc, 36 Soho Square, London W1D 3QY

www.bloomsbury.com

A CIP catalogue record for this book is available from the British Library

ISBN 978 0 7475 9741 4
10 9 8 7 6 5 4 3 2 1

Typeset by Hewer Text UK Ltd, Edinburgh
Printed by Clays Ltd, St Ives Plc

The paper this book is printed on is certified independently in accordance with the
rules of the FSC. It is ancient-forest friendly. The printer holds chain of custody

Mixed Sources

Product group from well-managed
forests and other controlled sources
www.fsc.org Cert no. SGS-COC-2061
© 1996 Forest Stewardship Council

For the soldiers, sailors, airmen,
special forces and civilians who gave their lives
for our country in the years 1939 to 1945

CONTENTS

The whole earth is the tomb of heroes, and their story is not graven in stone over their clay, but abides everywhere, without visible symbol, woven into the stuff of other men's lives.

Inscription on the Scottish National War Memorial
Edinburgh Castle

Preface

When I wrote a book, published in 2007 as *Courage: Eight Portraits*, I focused on men and women – among them Dietrich Bonhoeffer, Martin Luther King, Nelson Mandela and Aung San Suu Kyi – who, in the service of great causes and high ideals, had shown strength and determination which often led them to persist for years in dangerous courses of action when easier options were available. Their struggles against some of the greatest evils of the twentieth century demanded of them a particular kind of courage, one defined by the American scholar Frank Farley as 'sustained altruism'.

But as I commented in the introduction to that book, such courage is only part of a greater story. I wanted also to write about another and much more widely known form of courage: that required in wartime of soldiers, sailors and airmen, and of those who went behind enemy lines, and also of the many who stayed at home – civilians on the home front, some of whom were called to perform deeds every bit as brave as those required in the fiercest combat.

In this book I celebrate wartime courage, and the heroism of a generation that is now fading from our midst just as surely as its great predecessor generation, that of the First World War – now almost completely gone.

The Second World War, and the great events that unfolded over its six-year course, delivered its own generation of heroes, and on a huge scale. Hundreds of thousands of young people set aside their peacetime expectations of education, of learning a trade or profession, of starting a family, and instead swelled the ranks of the armed forces. Many thousands never returned. More than sixty years later it is difficult to comprehend the sheer scale of the nation's involvement in total war; the way in which the life of every family was touched, not seldom by tragedy; the innumerable individual acts of bravery and sacrifice recorded in service files and public citations; and the countless other instances of valour that went unrecorded or witnessed.

I wrote this book because I wanted to try to understand more of wartime courage, and of the experience of that generation in a conflict that ranged around the world. I am grateful to all those who have helped make it possible.

The chiefs of our armed forces have been generous in their suggestions and advice. Sir Richard Dannatt kindly wrote to me about the life of Stanley Hollis VC and others. I owe much to accounts by relatives and friends of the men and women I write about. Many organisations have been helpful in the research of this book. In particular I would like to thank the British Library, Dumfries Academy, the Green Howards Museum, the Soham Community History Museum (for historical accounts researched and written by Donna Martin) and the Victoria Cross Society. The distinguished Second World War historian Sir Martin Gilbert has been an unfailing source of advice and information, and he and his wife Esther have encouraged me greatly in the work. In particular his maps have added an extra dimension to the book and will greatly help the reader. Alex Canfor-Dumas has contributed a great deal by locating important new material from a wide range of sources; and once more Cathy Koester has assisted with painstaking research. Colin Currie has edited much of my work, redrafting and completing many chapters, especially over the last year. Bill Swainson has been an attentive and understanding editor. I thank him and his colleagues at Bloomsbury.

Sarah, my wife, has been a great source of support to me as I worked. And I have written these accounts of wartime courage not just to pay tribute to a passing generation, but in the hope that my young sons, John and Fraser, will one day read this book, and realise how much their world owes to the heroism and the sacrifices of the British people in the 1939–45 war.

Legend:

- ◒ Joseph Antelme
- ☐ Geoffrey Appleyard & Graham Hayes
- ▼ John Bridge
- ○ Charles Coward
- ■ Harry Errington
- △ Jane Haining
- ▲ Stanley Hollis
- ▽ Eric Liddell
- ◪ Leslie Manser
- ● Derek & Hugh Seagrim
- ◆ William Slim
- ◪ Richard Stannard & Godfrey Place
- ◓ Violette Szabo

SCOTLAND

Loch Cairnbawn
Aberdeen
Arisaig
ISLE OF MULL
Inveraray
Sterling
Kirkcaldy
Glasgow
Paisley
Edinburgh
ARRAN
THE BORDERS
Dunscore
Dumfries
Blyth
Sunderland

North Sea

Redcar
Middlesbrough
Loftus
Richmond
Stamford Bridge
Linton-on-Wharfe
Leeds
Collingham
Southport

Irish Sea

Manchester
Culcheth
Sheffield
Stoke-on-Trent
RAF Skellingthorpe
RAF Swinderby
RAF Conningsby
RAF Cottesmore
NORFOLK
Whissonsett
Norwich
ENGLAND
Birmingham
RAF Tempsford
Cambridge
Harwich
Moor Park
Radlett
London
Edmonton
Runnymede
Eltham
Sandhurst
Brookwood
Camberley
Beaulieu
Poole
Bournemouth
Devonport
Brixham
Portland
Falmouth
Plymouth
Dartmouth

WALES

Bristol Channel

English Channel

FRANCE

© Martin Gilbert 2008

0 kilometres 100
0 miles 50

Introduction

When I was growing up in Kirkcaldy in the 1950s and early 1960s, the observance of Remembrance Day each November mattered a great deal. With the end of the Second World War only a decade or so before, and with many of those present having lost spouses, friends, family members or close comrades, the solemnity of the occasion was still tinged with bereavement. It was as if the whole community had come together: representatives of the armed forces, youth organisations, veterans, the middle-aged and still-young members of the local British Legion, and others, in addition to the usual church-goers, for whom the occasion was a chance to remember someone who had not returned, to be consoled in a collective mourning the whole community could share.

More recently I have been privileged to attend each year the solemn act of national remembrance at the Cenotaph in Whitehall. The Second World War veterans are now much older; and along with them are younger men and women who have fought in the 'savage wars of peace' since that war's end, including Korea, and in the more recent conflicts in the former Yugoslavia, in Iraq and in Afghanistan. The poignancy of the two minutes' silence and the bugle call that signals its end is to me undiminished, and always I think again of those men and women standing at the war memorial in a town in Fife almost fifty years ago; and of the generation whose missing members they mourned – the 'greatest generation' as one American historian called them – and of what that generation sacrificed and achieved in the cause of freedom.

This book is a brief and sincere tribute to the men and women of Britain who endured the long years of the Second World War. As they grow older and fewer I believe their lives and deeds merit more attention, not less. Memories fade, but as archives are opened up, more information emerges – such as that contained in the personal files of the Special Operations Executive agents, which I found both fascinating and extraordinarily revealing. I hope the accounts that follow – the stories of a tiny sample of the sum total of the heroism of that generation – will serve it well, reminding succeeding generations of the dangers they faced and how they faced them, and of the huge debt we owe them still.

The Second World War was a vast conflict which ranged across oceans and continents and resulted in more than 50 million deaths. Great Britain, though dwarfed in size by the combined Axis powers, and the USA and the Soviet Union, was nevertheless the only major Allied power to be a combatant from the beginning of the war to its end. Its forces expanded hugely and the whole nation was mobilised for the exigencies of total war. More so than in the First World War, civilians were exposed to enemy action; and the worldwide scale of operations demanded great endurance and sustained courage from sailors, soldiers and airmen. Losses were heavy: nearly 400,000 British servicemen and servicewomen and 67,800 civilians died. In addition, more than 30,000 British merchant seamen lost their lives.

Given the vast scale of the British war effort, and the mass of evidence from the many thousands of official citations for the Victoria Cross, the George Cross, the George Medal, and other military and civilian distinctions, a short book such as this must, in attempting to portray wartime courage, reflect the difficulties that arise from the sheer wealth of material available. I have therefore tried in my selection to take account – however inadequately, and within the scope of this volume – of the nature of the war effort in terms of the main fighting services, civilians, and some less regular formations, and also of its range across space and time.

I begin with the stories of two VC-winning naval officers, both recognised for their heroic service in

Norwegian waters, though at different times and in very different circumstances. Richard Stannard, in peacetime a Merchant Navy officer with the Orient Line, commanded, as a Royal Naval Reserve lieutenant, the anti-submarine trawler HMS *Arab* towards the end of the ill-fated Norway campaign of 1940. Over four days, and under repeated air attack, he and his ship's company successively saved a French ammunition ship from disaster; rescued injured crewmen from another anti-submarine trawler; fought off repeated air attacks using highly effective new manoeuvres devised by Stannard; provided anti-aircraft cover for other warships by setting up of a cliff-top gun emplacement ashore; then, as British forces finally withdrew from Namsos, shot down an attacking Heinkel. Only weeks later Stannard was in action again, covering the cross-Channel rescue of British forces from Dunkirk: something he subsequently described as 'a picnic after Namsos'.

Much later in the war, in 1943, Godfrey Place, a young Royal Navy lieutenant, commanded *X-7*, one of six midget submarines that set out from a secret base in the northwest of Scotland to attack the German battleship *Tirpitz* in a heavily defended anchorage deep inside a Norwegian fjord. After a two-day 50-mile underwater approach through minefields and antisubmarine nets, only two of the midget submarines succeeded in their task of releasing their 2-ton high-explosive charges within range, and only those of *X-7* were positioned directly under *Tirpitz*. The damage they caused was sufficient to keep the battleship out of action for months, and she was never fully operational again. Of the eighteen submariners who set out on 'Operation Source', only six survived the war. The citation for Place's VC describes the hazards they faced in terms that fully explain such losses, and give us some idea of the seamanship, skill, ingenuity and sheer courage that enabled Place to press home his attack to the end.

John Bridge, a physics teacher turned mine and bomb disposal officer, served from 1940 until the end of the war and beyond, repeatedly practising his carefully acquired skills and knowledge in the most terrifying imaginable circumstances: defusing bomb after bomb, mine after mine, always aware that there were no second chances if things went wrong. His cool skills and unselfconscious courage, and his ability to teach and inspire the same in others, saved many lives; and on two occasions – in Sicily in 1943 and in Holland in 1944 – made it possible for crucial offensive operations, held up by unexploded enemy ordnance until he dealt with it, to proceed. He was one of only two mine disposal officers to be awarded the George Cross as well as the George Medal and Bar; and one of only eight people to receive both the George Cross and the George Medal. A thoughtful and methodical man, he used his ever-growing experience of enemy technology to assess each new challenge, preferably the night before it had to be tackled, and then sleep on it. His calm resolve in the face of such danger, again and again over years of war, is, to me, utterly impressive.

Graham Hayes and Geoffrey Appleyard of the Small Scale Raiding Force also faced great dangers again and again. Boyhood friends from Yorkshire, they served together over many months, carrying out daring and innovative actions: first against enemy shipping off Africa and later, as plans formed for the invasion of Europe, against strongpoints on the dangerous and heavily fortified shores of northern France, using their skills and sheer audacity to probe defences, take prisoners, and gain important intelligence, returning many times until their last venture together in September 1942. They developed new tactics in small-scale amphibious warfare; and, at a time when large-scale operations against occupied Europe were impossible, maintained the aggressive spirit, raised morale at home, and brought back much in the way of useful intelligence. By a sad coincidence, they died on the same day in 1943, but their innovative contribution to warfare left a significant legacy; the Small Scale Raiding Force they helped to establish is seen now as the precursor of the Royal Navy's elite Special Boat Squadron.

Leslie Manser, a flying officer with the RAF Volunteer Reserve, had just celebrated his twenty-first birthday when he took part in the RAF's first thousand-bomber raid on the night of 30/31 May 1942. He did not return. In the words of the citation for his posthumous VC: 'While the crew were descending to safety they saw the aircraft, still carrying their gallant captain, plunge to earth and burst into flames. In pressing home his attack in the face of strong opposition, in striving, against heavy odds, to bring back his aircraft and crew and, finally, when in extreme peril, thinking only of the safety of his comrades, Flying Officer Manser displayed determination and valour of the highest order.' He had taken off in an aircraft borrowed from a second-line squadron, of a type never regarded as successful, and which – though technically airworthy – did not perform well on the mission; but the imperatives of 'the big show' meant that many such aircraft flew that night. Manser could reasonably have returned to base when his aircraft's defects became evident, but he pressed on, reaching the target and dropping his bombs, before the successive failure of both engines and the subsequent fire meant the aircraft was doomed. At his parents' request his gravestone bears the words: 'He died to do his duty.'

When the news of that first thousand-bomber raid reached the Jews of the beleaguered Warsaw ghetto it was a welcome boost to morale there: it seemed perhaps that their Nazi oppressors were not invincible and would eventually be overcome. And to me some of the most heroic and inspiring stories I came across in researching this book were those of individuals who risked their lives as the Nazi regime sought to exterminate all of Europe's Jews.

Charles Coward, a British prisoner of war in the Stalag 8B camp near Auschwitz, used his position as a Red Cross liaison officer first to determine the appalling conditions endured by Jewish slave labourers in the adjoining Buna industrial complex, then to devise an unlikely and macabre plan that saved several hundred of them from certain death. Less well known, but no less noble, is the story of the group of ten British prisoners of war, who, in 1944, risked their lives to save that of a young Jewish woman, Sara Matuson. For many weeks they risked their lives, concealing her and caring for her 'like she was their little sister'. Thanks to them she survived.

Jane Haining, a Church of Scotland missionary in Budapest, sadly did not survive Nazi persecution. On leave in Scotland when war broke out in 1939, she returned immediately to her post and twice refused orders to go home to safety. As she wrote to her sister: 'If these children need me in the days of sunshine, how much more do they need me in the days of darkness?'

Working with Jews was a crime against Nazi law, and Jane was arrested, charged and taken to Auschwitz. She died there in the gas chambers in 1944.

While Europe remained under German occupation, the agents of SOE who organised and sustained the French resistance and undertook missions designed to support the planned Allied landings in Normandy faced terrible odds – a fact freely acknowledged in the earliest stages of their recruitment. Operating clandestinely in occupied territory, unprotected by the Geneva Conventions, and always vulnerable to betrayal, they risked their lives daily. Networks were insecure; capture, torture and death were the routine fate of many; and through 1943 and 1944 German countermeasures became more effective by the month. The service, heroism and sacrifice of SOE agents are now legendary. Of the many who served and died, two in particular stand out: Violette Szabo, a young war widow, and Joseph Antelme, a seasoned and wily operator whose skills had been honed in Indian Ocean commerce before the war. I believe their stories give us a precious glimpse into a twilight world of trust and betrayal, of nerveless courage and sudden escape, and a commitment to the higher goal of the liberation of Europe that never faltered even in the face of death.

And as D-Day, the date set for Operation Neptune – the largest amphibious landing in military history – approached, the risks and sacrifices necessary for success mounted steadily. Just hours before Allied forces began to land on their designated beaches – Utah, Omaha, Gold, Juno and Sword – a few heroic members of the Special Air Squadron staged a spectacularly successful diversionary attack, Operation Titanic. This involved a simulated mass aerial assault by paratroopers some miles south and west of Omaha Beach. It succeeded in drawing the main reserves of the defending forces there far back from what turned out to be the most hotly contested landing of all, that of the 1st and 29th US Infantry Divisions. Titanic is credited with making the crucial difference between success and failure at Omaha, but at a terrible price: only two of the ten SAS men involved survived.

On the same day and on the adjacent Gold Beach, where the British 50th Infantry Division fought its way ashore, there occurred one of the most striking examples of battlefield courage I came across as I worked on this book. Few, but very few, can rival the decisive and effective action in the searing heat of combat demonstrated by Company Sergeant Major Hollis of the Green Howards. For his determined and persistent heroism – storming a pillbox alone, overcoming its defenders and thus paving the way for a crucial advance to higher ground was just one of several acts of courage within a few hours – Hollis received the only VC awarded for action on D-Day.

Derek and Hugh Seagrim, two of the five sons of an eccentric Norfolk vicar, are unique as the only two brothers to have been awarded the Victoria Cross and the George Cross respectively. Lieutenant-Colonel Derek Seagrim led his infantry battalion in an attack on a strongpoint in the Mareth Line as Montgomery's Eighth Army advanced westward against Axis forces in North Africa in March 1943. Under heavy fire he led his men across an anti-tank ditch and single-handedly put two of the covering machine-gun posts out of action. His fearless and inspiring leadership in these actions, and in the defence of the forward positions thus established, resulted in the announcement of the award of his VC in the *London Gazette* of 13 May that year. Sadly, Derek Seagrim had died weeks earlier from wounds sustained in the subsequent battle of Wadi Akarit, the last major encounter in the victorious North African campaign.

Perhaps the most daunting and mysterious form of courage I encountered in working on this book was the kind that sustained individuals working on their own for years on clandestine operations far behind enemy lines. To me, its finest exemplar is Derek Seagrim's youngest brother, Major Hugh Seagrim GC, who campaigned in occupied Burma from 1942 until his death in 1944. Alone he maintained a British presence there, provided vital intelligence, and raised irregular forces – surrendering only when sustained Japanese brutality towards the Karens he led make surrender the right thing to do, and going to his death still arguing that his Karen comrades should be saved and he alone be executed.

The subject of the next chapter is a civilian: one who was famous before the war began. Eric Liddell, the phenomenally successful Scottish student athlete whose fame was spread worldwide by the film *Chariots of Fire* in 1981, won a gold medal at the 1924 Paris Olympics, graduated from Edinburgh University shortly afterwards, and never ran competitively again. A devout Christian, he had already determined that his future lay in mission work in China, where he worked first as a teacher in Tientsin and then, following his ordination, took responsibility in 1937 for a number of mission stations in an area of northern China where law and order were already breaking down as a result of international conflict between Japan and China. Returning from home leave in late 1940, Liddell continued his missionary work in circumstances of increasing difficulty. In 1941 Tientsin came under Japanese occupation, and in 1943, along with other enemy aliens, Liddell was consigned to an internment camp at Weihsien. All surviving accounts of life there describe Liddell's conduct and leadership – in circumstances of the steadily worsening deprivation and apparent hopelessness – in terms of near-saintliness. He died in captivity shortly before the end of the war. A memorial unveiled in 1991 bears a fitting biblical text: 'They shall mount up with wings as eagles; they shall run and not be weary.'

Well before the Second World War broke out the threat of mass aerial attack was recognised; and the concept of the 'home front' soon became brutal reality. But as the civilian population came under direct attack, heroes were soon discovered in its ranks too. From the many I learned of, it is possible to go into detail on only a few. The emergency fire-fighting force, the Auxiliary Fire Service, was severely tested early on, and in September 1940 one of its outposts, in London's West End, sustained a direct hit. In the ensuing chaos Harry Errington, a volunteer firefighter who by day worked as a tailor in Savile Row, rescued two of his comrades from certain death. Later in the war, in a little-known but potentially devastating incident, the details of which surprised me by their dramatic intensity, four civilian railwaymen saved a small town in Cambridgeshire from certain devastation in June 1944. Their response when a train laden with 400 tons of high-explosive bombs caught fire was disciplined, decisive and, in the face of terrible danger, it worked. But they paid a high price: one was killed instantly, and another died soon afterwards of his wounds. The town was saved. Benjamin Gimbert and James Nightall, the train's driver and fireman, were both awarded the George Cross, the latter posthumously.

However great the courage of those at the battlefront or behind the lines, and however great the combination of courage and leadership shown by such individuals as Stannard, Bridge and Derek Seagrim in bringing out the best in those who served under them, there is another form of courage essential to victory in the vastness of total war as waged from 1939 to 1945, and that is the courage required in high command – especially in adversity. Of the great British commanders in the Second World War, I believe that the modest, patient and reflective man from Birmingham who led the Fourteenth Army in Burma, General Sir William Slim, stands out for two reasons. In the words of the title of his incomparable memoir, he took his men from 'defeat into victory' – and he did so by his unique ability to train, motivate and lead them in ways that valued them in all their diversity; respected them; saw to their needs for supplies, support and medical care; and brilliantly restored their confidence and fighting spirit. Not for nothing did they call him 'Uncle Bill'. Led by him they went on to inflict upon the once invincible Japanese Army its most crushing defeat. The more I learned of Slim, the more his resilience, calmness and towering moral strength shone out. He serves us still as a model of military leadership in a democratic society.

I hope that in the following chapters the courage shown by these men and women – in its many forms and in widely varying circumstances – and the sacrifices they were called on to make, will be more clearly seen. And though I would not presume to explain their courage – upon which for a time the survival of our nation depended – I am in no doubt as to its significance, and will address that in the conclusion of this book.

I

Command under Pressure

Richard Stannard and Godfrey Place

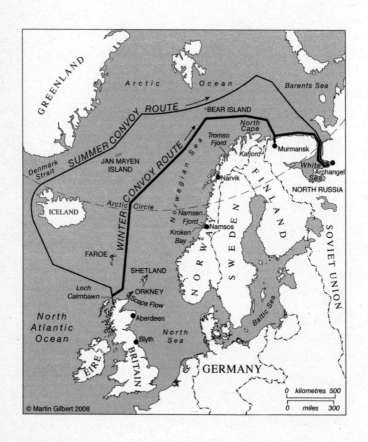

In 1940 the Royal Navy was a vast force. In its squadrons and flotillas in northern UK waters alone there were hundreds of warships, ranging from battleships and aircraft carriers, down through cruisers, destroyers and submarines to humbler vessels, such as those that made up the eleven impressively titled Anti-Submarine Striking Forces. In practice, each striking force consisted only of four ordinary steam trawlers: requisitioned by the Navy from their civilian owners, equipped with Asdic, depth charges and some defensive armament, and manned by fishermen and merchant seamen mainly conscripted 'for the duration'. One such trawler, part of the 16th Anti-Submarine Striking Force, was HMS *Arab*, commanded by Lieutenant R. B. Stannard, RNR, in peacetime a merchant navy officer with the Orient Line.

A citation in the *London Gazette* of 16 August 1940 begins: 'The King has been graciously pleased to approve the grant of the Victoria Cross to Lieutenant Richard Been Stannard RNR, HMS *Arab*, for outstanding valour and signal devotion to duty at Namsos', and ends: 'His continuous gallantry in the presence of the enemy was magnificent, and his enterprise and resource not only caused losses to the Germans, but saved his ship and many lives.' Stannard's was the first VC to be awarded to a Royal Naval Reservist in the Second World War; and the citation is all the more remarkable for the range and diversity of the feats of leadership and heroism it describes. For five days, and under repeated air attack, Stannard and his ship played a vital part in a rearguard action that, towards the end of an ill-starred campaign, covered the evacuation of British and French forces from central Norway.

Richard Stannard was born in 1902 in the seaport town of Blyth in Northumbria. When he was only ten his father, a master mariner, perished at sea in the North Atlantic. Along with his brothers, Richard thereafter attended the Royal Naval Merchant School, originally the Merchant Seaman's Orphan Asylum, founded in 1827 as a charity for the sons of seafarers lost at sea. In 1918 he followed his late father into the Merchant Navy as a cadet and advanced steadily, achieving the rank of second officer in 1928. In 1929, while serving with the Orient Line, he joined the Royal Naval Reserve as a probationary sub-lieutenant, and was promoted to lieutenant in 1937.

The Norway campaign of 1940 was brief and inglorious. Hitler had seized the country in a lightning invasion that began in early April and was aimed at acquiring advance naval and air bases for the Atlantic war and securing sea routes for strategic supplies, such as iron ore, from neutral Sweden. The Allied response, in support of the rapidly overwhelmed Norwegian Army, consisted of a poorly conceived and thinly spread seaborne invasion, mounted in mid-April by mainly British and French land forces with inadequate air support. The Allied invaders, not well organised, were also outnumbered. A total of 45,000 troops faced 80,000 Germans who were not only generally better trained and equipped; they had the crucial advantage of air superiority.

The Royal Navy, although dominant on the high seas, was throughout the campaign vulnerable when within the range of land-based enemy aircraft, of which there were many. Supporting and supplying the invading Allied forces took its toll. In the north, around Narvik – a port vital to exports from northern Sweden to Germany – British, French, and Polish forces held out until June; but a decision to evacuate the Allied bridgehead in the central Norwegian port of Namsos was made on 28 April, just two weeks after it had been established.

At 02.00 on that day HMS *Arab*, in company with trawlers of the 15th Anti-Submarine Striking Force, reached Namsos. Stannard's subsequent report on proceedings, dated 10 May 1940 and addressed to the Naval Officer in Charge, Aberdeen, is headed: 'A report on the Namsen Fjord actions, the embarking and disembarking of troops at Namsos, the manning of a shore defence position and experience gained against aircraft.' It is a terse and factual document that describes a complex series of sea- and land-based encounters, and includes observations about enemy tactics, comments on weapons and other equipment, and practical advice derived from coolly observed combat operations and set down for the good of the service. For instance, on avoiding hits from enemy bombers, Stannard advised:

> A mistaken idea is that zig-zagging is of no use with a speed below 13 knots. I consider that it was the saving of the *Arab* (maximum speed just over 12). By carefully watching the dive bombers and putting the wheel hard over after they had commenced to dive, it is very hard for them to hit a small ship, even at the height of 2,000 feet. After the first plane has dropped her bombs . . . bring the wheel hard over the other way.

With Stannard in command and developing such tactics, HMS *Arab* endured thirty-one air attacks in just four days: '24 by dive-bombers (2,000-3,000 ft.); 7 "High" (8,000/10,000 ft)'. The trawler sustained both damage and casualties, but survived and even fought back, bringing down on 2 May, the day on which she left Namsen Fjord, a Heinkel 115 ('the pilot of this machine seemed a novice. I decided to hold my fire until he was closer', Stannard wrote). The evacuation completed, HMS *Arab* then headed for brief safety in Scapa Flow: 'Proceeded well north, then south and west of Shetlands, arriving Scapa 1700 May 6th, Monday. Reported to Chief of Staff, watered and stored – 1900 – left Scapa.'

Although his retrospective report of 10 May is a truly impressive document that describes and draws important lessons from a near-continuous series of actions, Stannard can have had little opportunity for reflection at the time. Within an hour of their arrival on 28 April his crew were transferring stores from HMS *Carlisle* to a French Army *chasseur* unit, work that was interrupted within two hours by an air raid. Towards noon on the same day, when HMS *Arab* was next to *Saumur*, a French ammunition ship, in the harbour at Namsos, another air raid commenced. A 500lb bomb set fire to stores and an ammunition dump on the wharf next to the French ship. While another Royal Navy trawler manoeuvred to tow *Saumur* away from the immediate danger of an explosion, Stannard brought *Arab* as close as possible to the fire, its bow to the wharf and its engines running slowly, and for an hour – with the air raid still in progress – attempted to extinguish the flames. Meanwhile, the ammunition ship drifted out of control after a tow-rope had come loose and fouled her propeller. Stannard, having abandoned futile attempts at fire-fighting, took *Arab* alongside the French vessel, steadying her until the propeller was cleared.

Overnight *Arab* transferred hundreds of French soldiers from the dock to a transport ship, then proceeded out into the fjord to join other trawlers on anti-submarine duties, where the craft came under air attack; it was during this time that Stannard began to develop his carefully timed zig-zagging countermeasures. On the afternoon of 29 April, Stannard was ordered to find a sheltered spot in the shadow of a cliff to rest his crew, who had now been continuously on watch and frequently in action for forty-eight hours; but reports of a submarine sighting soon took them back to sea, and the afternoon found them under air attack again. That evening *Arab* provided anti-aircraft cover for the destroyer HMS *Bittern*, which early the following morning was the target of further heavy dive-bombing attacks, with *Arab* once more in the forefront of her defence.

By noon on the 30th, HMS *Gaul*, another anti-submarine trawler, had sustained serious damage when a bomb exploded on her bridge. Still under heavy bombardment, *Arab* evacuated *Gaul*'s wounded. Later that afternoon, when yet another air raid commenced, Stannard took bold and imaginative action against the Luftwaffe. With a bombing raid on the anti-submarine trawlers still in progress, he decided to establish anti-aircraft defences on top of the cliffs at Kroken Bay, where there were good fields of fire and a large cave at sea level that offered a safe lower base. Landing Lewis guns, ammunition, food and blankets, his men set up on the cliff-top a well-positioned gun-site, protected by machine-gun posts on its flanks and providing cover for Allied ships in the bay. French stores – including automatic rifles and a 60mm mortar and ammunition – that had remained on board from *Arab*'s first and interrupted task on the 28th were now appropriated for the new strongpoint. With *Gaul* and another trawler, *Aston Villa*, both out of action, their crews could now help in the manning of HMS *Arab*'s new position ashore.

Meanwhile, *Arab* herself was in danger. The main magazine of *Aston Villa*, lying close to her in the fjord and still burning following an air attack, might explode at any moment: a threat of which the CO of 16th Anti-Submarine Striking Force, Commander Congreve, was aware. When Stannard requested permission from him to board *Arab* and take her out of harm's way he was told: 'Keep away, it is too dangerous.' In the laconic terms of Stannard's report: 'Decided to take

Sub-Lieutenant Rees, RNVR, J. Nicholson and myself and try to save *Arab*. Cut lines and proceeded to move. Had moved 100 yards when *Aston Villa* blew up.' Then orders came that Namsos was to be abandoned. 'Commenced embarking wounded, stores, guns, and three crews on board *Arab*. Was told to do same with all despatch.'

Overloaded, and with bomb damage to her rudder and propeller sustained in an attack on the 29th, *Arab* set out down the fjord, transferred the wounded and the two other trawler crews to a larger Royal Navy ship, cleared Namsen Fjord and headed west. It was then that the attack by the He 115, whose pilot 'seemed to be a novice', began. With *Arab* raked by fire from the Heinkel's twin machine guns and ordered in plain language by its pilot to 'Go east or be sunk', Stannard played for time, answered ambiguously ('a suitable answer was sent in reply'), and waited as the Heinkel circled slowly closer, firing all the time. With the target on the beam and, at 800 yards, well within range, *Arab*'s Lewis guns and Oerlikon cannon suddenly opened up. The Heinkel fell into the sea.

Only weeks later Stannard was in action once again, this time in the Channel, while much of the British Army was being rescued from the beaches of Dunkirk – an experience he later described as a picnic compared to Namsos. The first anniversary of the outbreak of the war, 3 September 1940, found him at Buckingham Palace receiving his VC from King George VI at an investiture – the location for which, somewhat ironically, had had to be changed because of an air raid. In 1942, he received from the now exiled King of Norway the Norwegian War Cross for his actions in Namsos in April 1940.

Richard Stannard was promoted to Lieutenant Commander RNR and went on to serve with distinction in the Royal Navy in a number of theatres for the rest of the war. He was awarded the DSO for an action in February 1943 in the North Atlantic when, as captain of the destroyer HMS *Vimy* defending convoy SC 118, he played a major part in a pursuit which ended in the destruction of U187, a newly commissioned German submarine on its first patrol. In December 1944 he was honoured again, Mentioned in Dispatches for services in destroyers protecting convoys to northern Russia. The war over, he resumed his career with the Orient Line as chief officer and, from 1949, staff commander. Later he took up a post as marine superintendent of the P & O Line in Australia, retiring there and dying in Sydney, New South Wales, in July 1977.

The short-lived Norway campaign of 1940 was the last major incursion into mainland occupied Europe for some time, but in northern waters the Royal Navy continued to rule the waves. On the rare occasions the surface fleet of the much smaller Nazi *Kriegsmarine* took to the high seas, it risked and suffered losses, the most significant of which was the destruction of the *Bismarck* in the Eastern Atlantic in May 1941. Thereafter its major surface ships rarely ventured out, though their continued existence posed a threat to vital convoys and to the Royal Navy itself.

One such ship was *Tirpitz*, sister ship of *Bismarck*, and at over 41,000 tons the heaviest battleship ever built in Europe. Commissioned in 1939, *Tirpitz* was a fast, heavily armed and modern vessel, capable of doing immense damage as a commerce raider. By her mere presence in northern waters – she spent most of her career sheltering in the fjords of northern Norway – she acted as a constant menace to the Arctic convoys. And the possibility that she might, as the battleship *Bismarck* had done, break out into the Atlantic, forced the Royal Navy to keep scarce major warships – cruisers, battle-ships and aircraft carriers that might otherwise have played a vital role in the Far East – always within striking distance.

As a major threat, *Tirpitz* attracted the close interest of both the Navy and the RAF, and in the years 1943–44 more than a dozen operations were planned or mounted against her. In the first of these, Operation Source, the Navy's choice of craft for the attack could scarcely have been more different from the target. X-class 'midget' submarines were barely 50 feet long and just over 5 feet in diameter, with a displacement of 50 tonnes. And while *Tirpitz* had three high-pressure steam turbines delivering more than 160,000 horsepower, the main engine of the X-craft had originally been designed for a London bus.

Life in a midget submarine was not for the faint-hearted. Conditions aboard were grossly cramped, dirty and noisy, and their war role – to penetrate defended harbours and lay time-fused explosive charges of up to 4 tons directly under major enemy warships – demanded great skill, endless determination, and nerves of steel. Accordingly, the X-craft were manned only by volunteers who were already seasoned submariners. One such volunteer for 'special and hazardous duties' was a twenty-two-year-old lieutenant who had joined the Navy in 1935 at the age of fourteen.

Basil Charles Godfrey Place, known as Godfrey, was the son of Godfrey Place, a lawyer who had won both the DSO and the Military Cross in the First World War. Volunteering for submarines in 1940, Place served first as a liaison officer with the Polish submarine *Sokol*, then joined the 10th Flotilla in Malta, serving *Unbeaten* and winning a DSC for his part in the sinking of an Italian submarine in March 1942. His role in Operation Source on 22 September 1943 led to his capture and imprisonment as a POW; and eventually, in 1944, to the award of a VC.

In the summer of 1943, at Port HHZ, a secret base on Loch Cairnbawn in the remote northwest of Scotland, the volunteer crews in their newly delivered X-craft trained for their mission, practising approaches on large ships of the Home Fleet specially called in to act as targets; and preparing for the long and dangerous journey from Loch Cairnbawn to Kåfjord, a little inlet on Altafjord, 50 miles from the open sea on the northern coast of Norway, where reconnaissance flights had located and were regularly observing *Tirpitz* and two other heavy warships, *Scharnhorst* and *Lützow*.

On 11 September six X-craft set out for the thousand-mile journey. Each midget submarine had two crews: one for the passage out – on which they were towed by six larger submarines – and one operational crew to carry out the final attack. Two of the midget submarines broke adrift, one being eventually recovered, the other sinking with all hands. On 19 September the four remaining vessels approached the target area, still under tow. Towing problems delayed HM Submarine *Stubborn* and her charge *X-7* when a floating mine – part of the outer defences of Altafjord – became caught on the tow-line and was then impaled on the bows of the midget submarine. Place, the commander of *X-7*, went out on its forward casing and cleared the mine away with his foot.

Then a more hazardous phase of the operation began: a 50-mile underwater approach through minefields and anti-submarine netting in a narrow waterway studded with listening posts, lined with gun emplacements, and patrolled by anti-submarine craft. For two days the four remaining X-craft advanced up the fjord; probing, waiting, listening, proceeding with caution, negotiating hazard after hazard – at one point *X-7* struggled for an hour before freeing herself from anti-submarine nets – and all the time closing on their targets.

X-10 developed a defect and had to abandon the attack. On the final approach the German defences were alerted: *X-5* got within 500 yards of *Tirpitz* but was sunk by gunfire. *X-6*, commanded by Lieutenant Donald Cameron, and *X-7*, commanded by Place, alone remained. *X-6* was spotted on the surface and, with neither gyro-compass nor periscope functioning, in desperation, rammed *Tirpitz* and released both 2-ton charges of amatol explosive as close as possible to the target.

Now only Place in *X-7* remained in action, but had become entangled again in an anti-submarine net. Wriggling free once more, *X-7* surfaced at full speed, first colliding with *Tirpitz*, then sliding under her. Releasing one charge, then manoeuvring to release the other still under the target but far enough away from the first to inflict maximum damage, Place fulfilled his planned mission; then he found himself yet again entangled in a net, with air supplies running out and the time-fuses on the explosive charges already ticking.

Place was lucky as well as brave. When the first charge – one from *X-6* – went off it blasted *X-7* out of the clutches of the net. Suddenly the submarine surfaced, but, as Place later remarked: 'It was tiresome to find the *Tirpitz* still afloat.' *X-7* dived to avoid gunfire and waited; then, with compressed-air supplies now limited to only one more attempt at surfacing, surrender was the only option. *X-7*'s charges duly exploded. The six survivors of Operation Source spent the rest of the war in captivity.

The damage done to *Tirpitz* was substantial. All three propeller shafts were buckled and jammed, a 2,000-ton gun turret had been lifted from its mountings, and much of her radio, radar and other equipment knocked out. Not until April 1944 was she considered operational again, and then only in a limited capacity. In November of that year she was attacked by RAF Lancasters in Tromso Fjord. She sank with the loss of most of her crew.

After the war, Godfrey Place held no further submarine appointments. He transferred to the Fleet Air Arm, trained as a pilot, and experienced combat again, flying a Sea Fury naval fighter-bomber against Chinese fighters and land forces in the Korean War. Thereafter he commanded destroyers, an aircraft carrier, and a frigate; and was promoted rear-admiral in 1968, with duties as Admiral Commanding Reserves. He retired from the Navy in 1970 and died in 1994.

In a long, eventful and distinguished career, Godfrey Place served the Navy and his country well; but his finest contribution is that described in the joint citation for the award of the Victoria Cross to him and to Lieutenant Donald Cameron RNR:

> In the course of the operation these very small craft pressed home their attack to the full, in doing so accepting all the dangers inherent in such vessels and facing every possible hazard which ingenuity could devise for the protection in harbour of vitally important capital ships. The courage, endurance and utter contempt for danger in the immediate face of the enemy shown by Lieutenants Place and Cameron during this determined and successful attack were supreme.

2

Cool and Sustained Bravery

John Bridge

Whe Eighth Army captured Sicily in August 1943, and began to prepare for the invasion of the Italian mainland, it was clear that the necessary build-up of forces across the Straits of Messina would be slow. Vehicles had to be embarked from the beaches into landing craft because the retreating Germans had seeded the port of Messina with hundreds of depth charges. The fusing mechanism of these was unknown; the first attempt to determine it had killed five of a seven-man team, leaving the other two seriously wounded.

It was then that a slight, bespectacled, twenty-eight-year-old Royal Naval Volunteer Reserve lieutenant, fresh from harbour-clearance work along the North African coast, was put in charge of the operation. He found out all he could from interviewing the two survivors in hospital and, with a three-man team, then set to work in Messina harbour. John Bridge had defused his first bomb in 1940, after a brief familiarisation course and within only six weeks of joining the

Royal Navy. On his way out to the Western Desert in 1942 he had volunteered for a diving course in South Africa. In very difficult conditions, working at a depth of 40 feet, and backed up by more experienced divers, he used a controlled explosion to separate two of the depth charges which were then raised to the surface and hoisted on to the quayside. There he tackled the unknown mechanism, discovering a battery-operated fifty-two-day clock that could be set to anything from nought to fifty-two days, and disabled it.

In Messina harbour, still inexperienced but a determined diver, Bridge defied naval regulations and went down twenty-seven times in the following three days. Ordered to stop at noon on the third day, he worked on for two more hours to make the main harbour safe. Eventually he and his team disarmed 207 of the depth charges. 'I was the only one diving,' he later recalled; 'I had an assistant and several men working above water. My longest spell was twenty hours. I did not suffer particular discomfort, and never got tired. I left that to afterwards.'

The port of Messina was open for Allied warships and invasion barges on 2 September – not a moment too soon, as the assault on mainland Italy was scheduled to begin the following day. Soon larger ships could use the harbour and 1,500 vehicles a day were crossing the Straits, speeding the build-up of forces in Italy so effectively that the invasion force soon found itself three days ahead of schedule.

As a result John Bridge was awarded the George Cross, for 'the most conspicuous and prolonged bravery and contempt of death in clearing Messina Harbour of depth charges . . .'. In March 1945 Bridge attended an investiture at Buckingham Palace to receive his medal from the King , one of only two mine disposal officers to be awarded the George Cross, and the George Medal and Bar, and one of only eight people to receive both the George Cross and the George Medal.

Bridge's contribution to the early days of the Italian campaign was certainly significant, but it was only one of several over the course of the war. Before Messina he had served with distinction in England, during the Plymouth blitz and following raids on Falmouth docks; and in 1944 he went to Normandy, clearing mines and other explosives from beaches and battlefields. Then later in 1944, as the Allies advanced towards Germany, he saved a vital road bridge across the River Waal from attempted sabotage by German frogmen.

It is a truly awe-inspiring record of skill and determination, of sustained courage and unassailable calm in circumstances of the highest imaginable risk; yet in many ways John Bridge was an unlikely hero.

He was born on 5 February 1915 at Culcheth, a small town near Warrington in Cheshire. From Leigh

Grammar School he went up to King's College, London, gaining degrees in general science and in physics, then trained as a teacher. Prospects were limited, and in 1938 he applied for more than a hundred posts, and had a series of temporary jobs before becoming physics master at Firth Park Secondary School in Sheffield. When war broke out he was still teaching. This was not a reserved occupation; he knew that war service was inevitable and, like many of the generation brought up in the aftermath of the First World War, he did not assume that he would survive.

Bridge had a girlfriend and, as he put it more than sixty years later: 'I was interested from the moment I saw her. But the thought of getting married was out of the question. If you got married and you went to war, the chances were fairly high that you would be killed and your wife would be a widow. That's something we talked about.'

Following the outbreak of war, the Royal Navy established a register of names of suitably qualified science graduates. At the time of Dunkirk it advertised for men with honours physics degrees to work on bomb and mine disposal – a task that immediately appealed to Bridge, who later wrote: 'They could make use of my qualifications . . . and you helped to save lives.'

In June 1940 Bridge applied, was interviewed, and commissioned on the spot as a sub-lieutenant with the

Royal Naval Volunteer Reserve. He was measured for his uniform at Austin Reed in Manchester and the following week went to collect his uniform from the Regent Street branch in London, emerging properly dressed for what was to be a five-and-a-half-year career in bomb disposal.

Bridge joined a first contingent of only eight new bomb and mine disposal officers, most of them physics teachers from grammar schools. He was trained briefly: three and a half days on bombs with the RAF, and two and a half on mines with the Navy. It was his only formal training. On 2 July, as a bomb safety officer in the Plymouth–Falmouth area, Bridge defused his first bomb. During the following months, he and the teams under his command made safe more than a hundred unexploded devices. In December he defused a large bomb known to be fitted with a delayed-action fuse; for his calm courage on that occasion he was awarded the George Medal.

The following spring, between 20 and 22 March, as German bombing raids on Plymouth intensified, Bridge made safe fifteen bombs. One in particular, an unexploded bomb that threatened vital installations in Devonport dockyard, presented specific difficulties as it combined two types of fuse with an anti-handling mechanism. Bridge, largely self-taught but increasingly expert, worked for an hour – to the sound of the ticking of one detonator timer – in the knowledge that the bomb might go off at any moment. The problem was that the ticking timer could not be tackled directly without the other timer being disabled first. In a series of calculated risks, and in the nick of time, he succeeded. A King's Commendation for Brave Conduct followed.

In May 1941, after a raid on Falmouth, Bridge was called on to deal with a bomb lodged in a sluice valve chamber at the bottom of a 30-foot-deep shaft between two dry docks. Working alone in a space that offered no retreat, and where any mishap would have been instantly fatal, he secured the bomb to a winch that raised it out of 6 feet of water, and then disarmed it, thus saving equipment essential to the functioning of the dry docks. For his 'cold courage' he became the first naval officer to be awarded a Bar to a George Medal.

In his twelve months in the Plymouth–Falmouth area, Bridge dealt with 120 unexploded bombs, learning a great deal as he worked. Successive postings to Portland and the north of Scotland found him working mainly on mine disposal, 'and other jobs they gave me as well, so I had about three jobs there. I liked being busy. And fortunately, people could make use of my services.' His first foreign posting, to South Africa, followed. There he continued to work on mine disposal and, in the Simonstown naval base, taught mine and bomb disposal to other service personnel.

From South Africa he was sent to Egypt. There was some harbour clearance, but little else to do. That did not suit John Bridge, so he found a way out. A colleague due to be sent to the newly opened Italian front had personal reasons – concerning a girlfriend based in Egypt – for declining. Bridge, as ever, was looking for things to do, and succeeded in going to Sicily in his colleague's place. When he arrived there his first job, that of clearing Messina harbour, was to keep him very busy indeed.

Bridge recalled decades later that as soon as he had finished clearing the harbour:

The captain said to me, 'Bridge, the dry dock in Messina has not been used during the war. Can you get it into use again?' Well luckily for me, I had done an exercise earlier in the war when I was in Scotland, where I had to learn how a dry dock worked. So when the captain asked, luckily I knew how it worked. So I got that dry dock working in less than a week. If you have certain skills, and luck, use it.

Before the war ended he had further opportunities to utilise both his skills and his luck. He was in Normandy on 7 June 1944 – D-Day plus one – supervising the clearing of the beaches at Arromanches. By September

1944 he was clearing mines in the River Scheldt and the port of Antwerp. Late in the evening of 29 September, as he was about to go to bed, Bridge was suddenly ordered to Brussels and flown from there to Nijmegen in an Avro Anson – at under 100 feet for most of the way: 'the tops of the church spires seemed higher than us', he later recalled. 'The cows dashed frantically trying to get away from the frightening noise, and people looked up at this large machine skimming the roofs of their houses.'

On reaching XXX Corps HQ at Grave he was taken to be briefed by General Horrocks, whose advance was being held up by daring German attacks on nearby road and rail bridges over the River Waal. Horrocks explained the situation, then after learning that Bridge had not had breakfast, told his sergeant: 'Sergeant, get this officer some sandwiches. He will require them when he is working under the bridge.'

Twelve German frogmen, one of them a German swimming champion who had competed against the British team in the 1936 Berlin Olympics, had steered fused explosive charges downstream and lodged them against the bridge. One charge had gone off, blowing a 60-foot hole in the bridge; the other charges remained, however: hence the urgency of the summons from Antwerp. Bridge took to the water in an assault boat, and found a float attached to something underwater that could not be identified. 'What was it?' he later wrote. 'There was only one way to find out: get into the water and explore.' Bridge stripped to his underpants and dived in. By touch, using his bare feet, he identified a suspicious device and secured it so that it could be hoisted out of the water by engineers waiting on the bridge above. It was then lowered into his assault boat, where he defused it. On returning to England, Bridge was promoted to lieutenant commander.

A modest man, Bridge recalled years later the kindness of the very senior officer who had called for sandwiches to keep him going on his task. For his part, Bridge cared greatly about those for whom he was responsible. From the time of Dunkirk in June 1940 until when he left the Navy in March 1946, he led his teams with pride and care. 'My men got five George Medals and seven or eight British Empire Medals. And I never lost one man. Not one man was killed. And one person injured only, and that person was myself. I put that down to a certain amount of skill, and luck.'

Bridge led by example. 'You can't teach cool-headedness,' he explained. 'You just did it by leadership. You showed them how you did it, and they did it. And this is one of the things that I find very interesting: the number of brave men. There were a tremendous number of them. Courage means a lot to me.'

John Bridge's personal courage was immense; it was demonstrated time and time again throughout his service. How he managed to persevere under such intense and sustained pressure is a mystery, but an important element of it was his sheer professionalism. The man who did the 1940 short course with seven colleagues sought, over subsequent years, to master in every possible detail the technology of death that he had to confront each time he went to work on a mine or bomb. In Bridge's own words:

The more you know about a situation and plan to overcome it, the better. When I had a difficult job, I always worked out a solution the night before, before I went to sleep. So when it came to the crunch in Messina, I knew every move and the sequence in which to do it. So I felt no hesitation when it came to it. It's not foolhardiness. You've got to have the best possible chances of survival.

John Bridge survived and served, adding to his skills, leading his men, and – as he said of the consequences of his efforts at Messina – 'making a difference'. Throughout his naval career he showed courage of the highest order, with technical skills, leadership and modesty that matched that courage and enabled him to make the most of it.

Bridge's contribution in war was immense; when peace came he served again: first as an assistant education officer in Southport, becoming in 1963 director of education for Sunderland Borough Council, until he retired in 1976.

On 28 June 2006 John Bridge attended a reception given by the Queen at Windsor, joining his fellow George Cross and Victoria Cross holders. He died, at the age of ninety-one, the following December. His wife, Jean, whom he had married near the time of his visit to Buckingham Palace in 1945, and to whom he was devoted, died shortly afterwards. The fears they had discussed sixty years before – of a prolonged widowhood should he die in the course of his always perilous war work – had proved to be happily unfounded.

3

Ingenuity and Daring

Geoffrey Appleyard and Graham Hayes

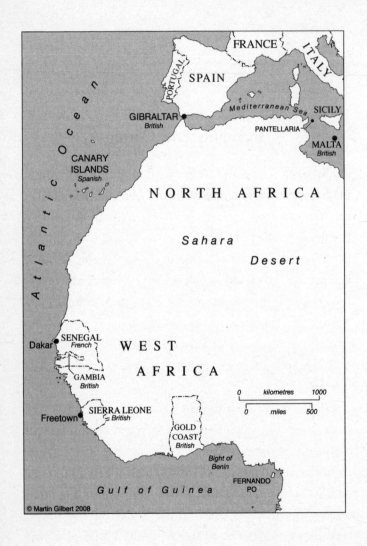

FRANCE

ITALY

PORTUGAL

SPAIN

Mediterranean Sea

SICILY

Atlantic Ocean

GIBRALTAR
British

PANTELLARIA

MALTA
British

CANARY
ISLANDS
Spanish

N O R T H   A F R I C A

Sahara

Desert

Dakar

SENEGAL
French

W E S T   A F R I C A

GAMBIA
British

Freetown

SIERRA LEONE
British

GOLD
COAST
British

kilometres   1000
0

0   miles   500

*Bight of
Benin*

FERNANDO
PO

Gulf of Guinea

© Martin Gilbert 2008

As I read about the Second World War, I was struck again and again by how often individuals made a difference; and how their courage – whether in the heat of battle or in longer struggles such as those in bomb disposal or in covert operations behind enemy lines – not only helped substantially in the long struggle against the Axis powers, but inspired others. A few, very few, through their courage and innovation, managed to change official thinking on the role and use of *irregular* operations and, by their example and bold initiatives in training, brought to the fore a new and effective form of warfare.

Geoffrey Appleyard and Graham Hayes grew up as close friends in the village of Linton-on-Wharfe in Yorkshire in the 1920s. When war came, Appleyard was commissioned into the Royal Army Service Corps (RASC), Hayes into the Border Regiment. Together they would help form the Small Scale Raiding Force, established under the authority of the Chief of Combined Operations, Admiral Lord Louis Mountbatten, and the precursor of the Royal Navy's elite Special Boat Squadron. Their exploits in 1942 and 1943 harassing Axis forces and assets from the English Channel to the Gulf of Guinea combined audacity with economy of force, created fear and uncertainty for the enemy, and served to raise morale at home. Appleyard and Hayes both won the Military Cross, and Hayes a Distinguished Service Order. Neither survived the war, and, by a sombre coincidence, and hundreds of miles apart, they died on the same day in 1943. Hayes is buried in a well-tended grave near Paris. Appleyard's remains have never been found: his name is inscribed on the Cassino memorial to the missing in Italy.

Appleyard was born in 1917 to some privilege. The son of a Leeds motor-trade entrepreneur, in school he excelled at sport but worked for exams when it was absolutely necessary, doing well enough to gain a place at Cambridge. There too he excelled, as an oarsman and a skier, becoming captain of boats for his college and leading the English skiing team to unexpected victory in the Anglo-Norwegian meeting held over the Easter vacation in 1938. To the astonishment of his sporting friends, a belated burst of study in his final term resulted in a first-class degree in engineering. Later he said that meant less to him than his skiing Blue.

In 1938, Appleyard joined his father's firm, working with the mechanics on the shop floor, at first as 'the man who passes the tools to the man who passes the tools', but intent on learning all he could about what was then known as 'motor repair'. As Britain prepared for war Appleyard was a natural for the RASC supplementary reserve list of officers, and even before joining up he helped train hundreds of Territorial Army motor mechanics.

Mobilised in 1939, Appleyard led an RASC motor-repair mobile workshop and spent the period of the 'phoney war', from September that year, in northern France. When the German Army broke through and the retreat to Dunkirk accelerated, he was shocked by an order to destroy all the vehicles he had so carefully maintained; he did, however, get all his men safely to the beaches and almost all of them home; he himself was among the last to make it.

Back in England, and irked by inactivity, Appleyard volunteered for 'No. 62 Commando', a covert unit within SOE, and the predecessor of the Small Scale Raiding Force. This commando unit had been established by Churchill three days after Appleyard returned from Dunkirk, with a note to the Chiefs of Staff: 'The passive resistance war, which we have acquitted ourselves so well in, must come to an end.'

Appleyard was accepted – because of his skiing and rowing, he thought – and loved the life. Writing home he described it as '. . . absolutely terrific', and 'the grandest job in the army . . . a job that if properly carried out can be of enormous value'. His immediate superior, Major Gus March-Phillipps, was a brave and charismatic officer, who would have a huge influence on Appleyard's war, and – through Appleyard – on that of Graham Hayes.

After training in Arran, Appleyard found the action he sought, in a daring operation in which HM Submarine *Tigris* took him and another man to land in collapsible canoes south of the Loire estuary to pick up two agents from occupied France. One canoe was holed on landing and the agents did not turn up until the presence of the submarine offshore was about to be betrayed by moonrise. Across a couple of miles of heavy seas, with four in a canoe designed for two, Appleyard made it back to the submarine, where naval officers pronounced that he 'wasn't such a bad sort for an army man'. Lieutenant (acting Captain) John Geoffrey Appleyard, RASC, was awarded a Military Cross.

By then, Hayes too was a junior officer in the army, though by a very different route to that of his boyhood friend. Leaving his home village not long after he left school, he went to sea, spending a year on merchant ships, eventually reaching Australia in a square-rigged sailing ship, and coming back around the world. In the late thirties he set up a furniture business but left it to join the army, first as a sapper with the Royal Engineers, then graduating via an Officer Cadet Training Unit to become an infantry lieutenant with the 1st Battalion, the Border Regiment.

An MI5 memo on Hayes's personal file, dated August 1941, reads in relation to a possible secondment: 'Reason for enquiry: for employment as a member of crew on a ship . . .', then: 'Action taken: to be specially employed.' The 'ship' concerned barely qualified as such: the *Maid Honour* was a 65-ton Brixham trawler – a sailing vessel with a small auxiliary engine. The summons to Hayes to join her had been initiated by her freshly appointed second-in-command, Geoffrey Appleyard, with the approval of her commander, Captain Gus March-Phillipps. *Maid Honour* was the unlikely flagship of the newly formed seaborne commando unit, known as Maid Honor Force, which reported to Mountbatten – whose idea it was – in the Special Service Department of the War Office.

Fitted out and commissioned in a quiet corner of Poole harbour, the former trawler, a wooden fishing boat of innocent appearance and at no risk from magnetic mines, and her crew had been given a truly daunting task: that of sailing across the Bay of Biscay, rounding West Africa and operating on the coasts of the Gulf of Guinea, by then largely hostile territory; once there, Maid Honour Force would report on enemy submarine activity and carry out clandestine raids on whatever might be worth raiding. The trawler left for her mission in August 1941, and was to do damage that utterly belied her modest size and origins.

Appleyard's letters indicate that his high hopes of 'the grandest job in the army' were not disappointed. Commander, second-in-command and first mate (March-Phillipps, Appleyard and Hayes respectively) got on well, both professionally and socially. Appleyard's early reports from a British base near Freetown are typically enthusiastic: he notes that there are other Yorkshiremen in the mess, including a man from Linton; there is swimming, diving and spear-fishing; and he is busy – 'It's funny, but it seems that the smaller the ship is the more there is to do on it.'

Maid Honour served on the West African coast for six months, but had to be abandoned there in 1942 as she was too unseaworthy to return home. But she served her purpose, demonstrating the value of seaborne special operations and thus resulting in the establishment of the Small Scale Raiding Force and its subsequent expansion.

The highlight of the force's time off Africa was an astonishing action in early 1942. For Operation Postmaster, the Brixham trawler approached the harbour of Fernando Po, a Spanish island in the Gulf of Benin off the coast of West Africa – technically neutral territory. Intelligence reports had indicated the presence of high-value Axis shipping, which turned out to be the Italian cargo liner the *Duchessa d'Aosta* and two German cargo vessels. On the night of 14/15 January, Appleyard led an assault party tasked with taking over the liner. There were problems along the way: as they approached, an incident led to Appleyard having to leap an 8-foot gap over water, but he succeeded. Then the first charge he laid to sever the ship's anchor chain failed to go off, but, ignoring the usual safety precautions, he immediately set another, which worked.

Appleyard took over as second-in-command of the liner and, in the words of the subsequent citation, 'displayed initiative and ability to command, under circumstances of great difficulty, of a very high order indeed' – a remarkable achievement for someone who had started the war in command of a motor-repair unit and was still a fairly junior army officer. *Maid Honour* and her team had proved their worth. March-Phillipps was awarded a DSO, Appleyard a bar to his MC, and Hayes an MC. Before his investiture at Buckingham Palace, Appleyard, whose experience of formal drill in the RASC and the special forces was negligible, was carefully prepared ('Advance three steps. Halt. Bow. Stand to attention. Bow. Retreat one step. Right turn. Quick march') by his younger brother, a cadet with the Leeds University OTC.

In March 1942, with Europe still under Nazi occupation, March-Phillipps, Appleyard and Hayes were posted to Poole to prepare commandos for the new Small Scale Raiding Force. Forming a part of Special Services Command and equipped with powerful 30-knot motor launches, the unit trained to carry out raids against enemy forces on the coasts of France. Training routines were rigorous and sometimes extreme, with exhaustion, immersion, seasickness and gruelling exercises involving live rounds and mines to prepare the men for the dangers they would face in action.

March-Phillipps and Appleyard reflected on their experience and together – and most irregularly – wrote a paper on discipline and morale and sent it to their superiors in British Army Command. It made important points about the wide gap between conventional training and combat; and contrasted the experience of the First World War – then well within living memory – in which many soldiers had seen action again and again, with that of 1942, when retreats around the Mediterranean and disasters in the Far East had been followed by the need to train at home, for years and virtually in peace-time conditions, for the coming liberation of Europe. 'That is why we are pushing for a more aggressive policy,' they wrote, 'a really whole-heartedly adopted policy of small scale raiding' – one that would give more soldiers 'at least a taste of action, a baptism of fire'.

And they practised what they preached. March-Phillipps, Appleyard and Hayes led persistent and daring raids, landing by small boat from their motor launches and repeatedly harassing enemy forces in Brittany and Normandy with small but unpredictable incursions that compelled the defenders to reinforce their guards and sentries along hundreds of miles of coastline, thus diverting significant numbers of troops from war duties elsewhere. Appleyard wrote home about 'another successful little party the night before last . . . this time we brought back seven prisoners'. And in a raid on the Casquets lighthouse, a German naval signal station off Cherbourg ('a notoriously evil place . . . a tremendous tide race round the rocks . . .'), they captured all present and returned with invaluable codebooks and other naval documents. Mountbatten, by then Chief of Combined Operations, sent a telegram of congratulations.

Dangerous and demanding though their work was, it was good while it lasted. In all Appleyard and Hayes carried out as many as twenty such operations. But on the night of 12/13 September 1942 the three set out on another raid on St Onorine-des-Perts, a small coastal village near Cherbourg: a raid that went disastrously wrong. Appleyard should probably not have been there. An ankle injury sustained in a previous raid meant that he could not go ashore, or even walk unaided; but his skill as a motor-launch navigator in such treacherous conditions – close inshore on a rockbound coast in pitch darkness – meant that he could still contribute. Hayes, March-Phillipps and seven others went ashore in a small canvas-sided, wooden-bottomed collapsible boat. They came under fire as soon as they landed, fought back, but were overwhelmed. Appleyard drew as close as he could in the launch to provide covering fire, but no targets could be identified. The shooting died down and Appleyard heard a voice, he thought that of Hayes, telling him to save his ship and go away because all was lost. With one of his two engines out of action following a hit, and still under fire from the shore, Appleyard had no option but to retreat. Next morning the launch was escorted into Portsmouth with air cover provided by Spitfires.

March-Phillipps was dead, killed as he and his men had tried to get back to the boat; the rest were either dead, or wounded and captured – apart from Hayes, who was later posted missing but had in fact escaped. He had taken to the water, swum for his life, and been washed ashore along the coast. A French farmer took care of him, then passed him on to the underground networks that looked after Allied personnel on the run in France. From Normandy he was spirited first to Paris and then to the Spanish border. News of his escape reached his parents back in England, but his freedom was soon cut short: the local Spanish police handed him back to the Germans, and he was taken to Fresnes prison near Paris. While he was there, on 19 February 1943, his brother, Flying Officer Malcolm Cedric Hayes, RAFVR, was shot down near Saumur, fifty miles away, and killed.

Appleyard, having lost both an esteemed commanding officer and his best friend in a single night, was devastated; but he took on the temporary command of the Small Scale Raiding Force and soon resumed operations, capturing in one raid 'the most useful prisoner obtained by anyone up to date . . . very chatty and nothing is too much trouble for him to describe in detail'. It was indeed a coup; and Appleyard was summoned to London to meet Churchill, General Sir Alan Brooke, the Chief of the Imperial General Staff, and Admiral Sir Dudley Pound, the First Sea Lord. The contribution of the Small Scale Raiding Force to the war effort was confirmed and its further expansion planned. Awarded a DSO, Appleyard went to Buckingham Palace for a third investiture in eleven months. The King was amused as well as impressed: 'What, you again?'

As Allied forces prepared in 1943 for the liberation of German-occupied Europe, Appleyard, with his unique experience and understanding of seaborne special operations, was increasingly in demand. British successes in North Africa led to Operation Husky, the invasion of Sicily, for which detailed reconnaissance of landing places and enemy strongholds was required. Promoted to major, Appleyard was sent to Malta, from where he reconnoitred the island of Pantelleria, halfway between the African shore and Sicily. Leading a small group landed from a submarine, he carried out a thorough survey of its defences, took the usual prisoners, and returned to Malta to report his findings. The capture of Pantelleria was achieved soon after. It marked the first step in the liberation of Europe.

Landings on Sicily began on 9 July 1943. On the evening of 12 July Appleyard requested permission to go on a flight with commandos who were to be parachuted in to protect a vital bridge near Randazzo in the east of the island. He did so to ensure the drop zone was the right one, and to check on where reinforcements should go in the following night. The Albemarle aircraft, with ten paratroopers and Appleyard on board, took off later that evening. He had told his unit he expected to be back around 1 a.m. on the 13th. He never returned; all on board the aircraft were posted missing, presumed dead. On the same day, the 13th, after nine months in solitary confinement, Graham Hayes was taken out of his prison cell at Fresnes and executed by his German captors.

Hayes was buried in the grounds of the prison where

he was shot. Later his body was taken to the Commonwealth War Graves Commission cemetery at Viroflay, 4km east of Versailles, where he is one of three soldiers buried with seventy British, Canadian, Australian and New Zealand airmen. No trace was ever found of the Albemarle or of those who flew in it. The two boys who had grown up together in Linton had fought together against a vile tyranny that had conquered Europe and would in its turn be conquered. Although they did not live to see the Allied victory, their remarkable bravery, ingenuity and selfless determination in a new form of warfare brought the defeat of the Axis powers closer.

In the now deconsecrated church in Linton, near Wetherby in Yorkshire, there was once a stained-glass window that commemorated them; today the church is a private dwelling, and the memorial window has gone. But in the neighbouring village of Collingham, there is a memorial hall originally dedicated to those who fell in the First World War. Within it a small brass plaque commemorates also those who died in 'The Second Great War'. On it are the names of Geoffrey Appleyard and Graham Hayes.

4

Press Home Your Attack

Leslie Manser

© Martin Gilbert 2008

The night of 30/31 May 1942 was a momentous one for RAF Bomber Command; under its new commander-in-chief, Air Marshal Sir Arthur Harris, it carried out the first ever thousand-bomber raid. This represented not just a major change of tactics; it set the pattern for a series of devastating attacks against Germany's major cities and industrial heartlands that lasted until the end of the war. That night in May, 1,047 bombers of seven different types, carrying 1,500 tons of mainly incendiary bombs, took off from airfields all over southern England and headed for Cologne.

Of the 1,047 that set out, forty-one did not return. Among them was a Manchester heavy bomber of 50 Squadron, captained by Flying Officer Leslie Manser, who pressed home his attack in a disabled aircraft capable of flying only at dangerously low levels; nursed it back towards safety – despite flak damage, onboard fire and the loss of an engine; and who died attempting to ensure that his aircrew could escape as it plunged to the ground. His posthumous VC was announced in the *London Gazette* on 20 October that year.

Leslie Manser, who died only a few days after his twenty-first birthday, was born in 1921 in New Delhi, India, where his father, Thomas Manser, worked as an engineer in the Post and Telegraph Department. When Leslie was still quite young his family returned to England, settling in Radlett, Hertfordshire. He was educated at schools in Cambridge and Hertfordshire. The RAF was not his first choice for a career in the services: he had attempted to join both the Army and the Navy before being accepted for pilot training in August 1940. After initial training he was commissioned as a pilot officer in May 1941, completed navigational and operational training in the following months, and joined 50 Squadron, then flying Hampdens, at RAF Swinderby in Lincolnshire, one of the last airfields to be opened under the RAF's pre-war expansion plans.

In his first few months at Swinderby he flew in sorties over Frankfurt, Berlin, Hamburg and Karlsruhe. His superior flying skills were spotted early, and for several months he served as an instructor with 14 Operational Training Unit, RAF Cottesmore, before returning in April 1942 to 50 Squadron. By then 50 Squadron had relocated to RAF Skellingthorpe – also in Lincolnshire – and had begun the transition from Hampdens to the newer and much heavier Manchester bomber.

The Manchester had a short and undistinguished history. Twelve hundred were ordered from Avro but only 200 were delivered, the rest being cancelled. Designed around a vast bomb bay, and first flown only six weeks before war was declared, the Manchester rapidly acquired a reputation for exceptional unreliability. The main problem was the choice of engine. The Rolls-Royce Vulture was of innovative layout: two V-12 engines joined at the crankshaft to make an 'X-24'. But the resulting power output was disappointing, and the lubrication system unreliable, so that production of the Vulture engine was soon dropped in favour of the far superior Merlin. Perhaps the only redeeming aspect of the generally regrettable Manchester was that a development of it − powered by four Merlins rather than two Vultures, and known as the Lancaster − became by far the best heavy bomber of the war. However, early in the war the demand for heavy bombers was such that some Manchesters remained in front-line service, though by 1942 many of them had been relegated to the training role.

Manser's first mission in a Manchester was to drop leaflets on German-occupied Paris on 8 April 1942. A series of operational sorties with 50 Squadron followed. The young pilot officer, already distinguished by his early contribution as an instructor with an operational training unit, consolidated his reputation both as an airman and as a leader, and was promoted to the rank of flying officer on 6 May.

Arthur 'Bomber' Harris is now a controversial figure. His mass raids – the 'area bombing' of German cities between May and December 1942 – were criticised during the war on moral grounds, and after it in pragmatic terms, when the strategic bombing survey showed that their impact on war production had initially been limited. In them Bomber Command suffered heavy losses in human, material and financial terms. But in 1942, with Europe under Nazi domination, the Soviet forces in the East desperately needed whatever interventions the Western Allies could bring to bear.

Only area bombing – however costly – offered a means of significant attack against Germany; and from its outset it imposed upon the enemy a huge defensive commitment of guns, aircraft and manpower that would otherwise have been available for offensive action against the Soviet Union. Later in the war, from the time of the Casablanca directive of January 1943, area bombing gave way to more accurate and effective strategic bombing. Improvements in tactics, bomb-sights, navigational techniques, and fighter protection made Allied bombing more precise and destructive, and vastly decreased Germany's ability to wage effective war.

The Bomber Command that Harris took over early in 1942 was not only costly; it was also seen as inefficient. Post-raid analyses had shown that more than 90 per cent of bombs fell more than 5 miles from their target. Harris, at a time when the very existence of his Bomber Command was under threat, approached Churchill and the Chief of Air Staff, Sir Charles Portal, with a plan he believed would increase the effectiveness of raids on Germany and might diminish their losses too. The result was the first thousand-bomber raid, scheduled for May 1942 and codenamed Operation Millennium.

Harris was a determined and forceful character who, when the raid was first planned, had only slightly more than 400 fully operational bombers in front-line squadrons. To make up his thousand he intended to use aircraft from Training Command; he also approached Coastal Command, whose bombers were allocated to a maritime role in support of the Royal Navy, and whose commander initially agreed to provide 250 aircraft. However, shortly before the date of the planned raid, the Admiralty vetoed that: the battle against German U-boats – causing massive destruction of Allied shipping in the Atlantic – had first claim on these aircraft, and to concede them to Harris's 'big show' would not only be unacceptable in the short term; it would set a dangerous precedent.

It was an inter-service tussle that Harris could not win; so to make up his numbers he reached deeper into the RAF's own resources – for men and aircraft. Not every pilot on Operation Millennium would be fully trained; in one bombing group forty-nine aircraft – nearly a quarter – were flown by pupil pilots, some still in the earlier stages of training. Training squadrons were compelled to give of their aircraft too, though not all of these were in fully operational condition. For the sake of the first thousand-bomber raid, and perhaps even for the future of Bomber Command, Harris was uncompromising. The 'big show' must go on, so men and aircraft had to be found.

Manchester L7301, accepted by the RAF in December 1940, was an early model. Only the twenty-eighth Manchester to be built, it had never seen front-line service. Doubts about its reliability led to its being kept in storage until it could be modified to later production standards, but it was eventually taken on by 106 Conversion Flight for second-line duties. On the morning of 30 May 1942, Flying Officer Manser went to RAF Coningsby, collected L7301 from 106 Flight, and flew it back to Skellingthorpe. The aircraft was grubby inside, lacked an upper turret, and its rear escape hatch could not be opened. However, in the circumstances, and since it was officially airworthy, it was loaded with 2½ tons of 4lb incendiary bombs and prepared for the night's raid. That preparation included knocking a hole in the fuselage to accommodate the air gunner normally positioned in the upper turret.

The final target for Operation Millennium was chosen only at midday on 30 May, less than twelve hours before the first planes were due to take off. The original choice, the city of Hamburg, with its great port and shipyards that were building a hundred U-boats a year, was ruled out because of poor local weather conditions; Cologne, Germany's third largest city (though not a major centre of war production), was substituted. Final preparations began. A message from Harris was read out to all the aircrew who would fly:

The force of which you form a part tonight is at least twice the size and has more than four times the carrying capacity of the largest force ever before concentrated on one objective. You have an opportunity, therefore, to strike a blow at the enemy which will resound, not only throughout Germany, but throughout the world . . . Press home your attack to your precise objective with the utmost determination and resolution in the foreknowledge that, if you individually succeed, the most shattering and devastating blow will have been delivered against the very vitals of the enemy. Let him have it – right on the chin.

Privately, Harris had already admitted to Churchill that up to 10 per cent of his thousand bombers might not return. Churchill said he was prepared for such losses.

The tactics used on Millennium were innovative, almost revolutionary. The big idea for the big show was the 'bomber stream'. The development of more accurate navigational aids meant that, for the first time, large forces could assemble and fly together on a pre-determined route to and from the target in relatively tight linear formation, maintaining separation by keeping aircraft at carefully calculated different heights. Such concentrations of intruders would overwhelm enemy fighter control, but the risk of collision under these conditions was as yet untested.

Manser took off from Skellingthorpe with the rest of 50 Squadron at 22.50 on 30 May. Problems were encountered almost immediately. The ferry flight from Coningsby that morning had been straightforward; but, with the additional load of incendiary bombs, the Manchester's Vulture engines began to overheat at 7,000 feet and it soon became clear that she would never reach the planned altitude of 12,000 feet. Despite this Manser pressed on, taking the sanguine view that Cologne's anti-aircraft 'flak' defences would be focusing mainly on the far more numerous attackers flying thousands of feet above him.

By 01.30 on the 31st, as L7301 drew near to Cologne much of the city was already on fire. Still at only 7,000 feet, Manser held his course straight and level despite his aircraft being caught in a searchlight cone and seriously damaged by heavy anti-aircraft fire. On reaching the designated aiming point, Flying Officer 'Bang On' Barnes released more than a thousand incendiary bombs. Manser then turned to head for home; just as he did so the Manchester received a further direct hit. Losing height to avoid the searchlights and further anti-aircraft fire did little good. At 800 feet, L7301 entered the range of 20mm tracer ground fire and was hit again.

Manser regained control and continued westward. Out of immediate danger, back in darkness, and still heading for home – though flying far lower than was ideal – his team checked for damage. The rear gunner had been slightly wounded by shrapnel, much of the rear bomb bay doors had been blown off, and the aircraft was difficult to control: problems, but nothing disastrous. Then, just as Manser coaxed the aircraft up to 2,000 feet, fire was spotted in the port engine, with flames from it reaching as far back as the tail. The outlook was suddenly much worse: an aircraft that had barely coped on two engines was now going to have to rely on one. The outlook was suddenly much worse.

Manser ordered his second pilot to activate the port engine's fire extinguisher; within ten minutes the flames diminished and then disappeared, but the added strain on the starboard engine soon began to show. In a last desperate effort to save the aircraft, all removable equipment was jettisoned, but that made no significant difference. The starboard engine overheated and would soon also fail amid flames. The brief operational life of Manchester L7301 was entering its final minutes.

Manser, Baveystock, Barnes, Horsley, King, Naylor and Mills – respectively the pilot, second pilot, bomb-aimer/navigator, wireless operator, second wireless operator and the two air gunners – prepared for the worst. The Manchester slowed to 110 knots, dangerously near its stalling speed. Manser, who knew that the aircraft would nose-dive as soon as he left the controls, gave the order for the crew to bale out. Baveystock attempted to persuade Manser to join the rest of them and abandon the aircraft; he even tried to attach a parachute to his skipper, but Manser refused it. The second pilot made it to the front escape hatch as the Manchester approached tree-top level, his parachute opening just in time to allow him a safe if watery landing in a ditch. He watched as Manchester L7301 crashed a few hundred yards away and immediately caught fire.

High above them the surviving British bombers, still numbering more than a thousand, made their way homewards, the dawn of 31 May breaking behind them. Wellingtons, Stirlings, Halifaxes, Whitleys, Lancasters, Hampdens and Manchesters dispersed in their squadrons and returned to their bases. The charred remains of L7301 lay in woodland at Molenbeersel near the Belgian village of Bree, three miles from the Dutch border, Manser within it. Barnes was soon captured and spent the rest of the war in a prisoner of war camp in Germany. The other five – Baveystock, Horsley, King, Naylor and Mills – were spirited away by sympathetic Belgians, and reached Liege two days later. They then successfully crossed France under the auspices of the Comet escape line before escaping through Spain to Gibraltar, from where they were flown home to England.

The crew's account of the conduct of their leader that night in due course resulted in the award of a Victoria Cross – as announced in the *London Gazette* that October – to 'Flying Officer Leslie Thomas Manser 66542 Royal Air Force Volunteer Reserve (Deceased) No. 50 Squadron'. Describing Manser's last mission, the citation ends:

While the crew were descending to safety they saw the aircraft, still carrying their gallant captain, plunge to earth and burst into flames. In pressing home his attack in the face of strong opposition, in striving, against heavy odds, to bring back his aircraft and crew and, finally, when in extreme peril, thinking only of the safety of his comrades, Flying Officer Manser displayed determination and valour of the highest order.

The first thousand-bomber raid had achieved limited success. Its contribution was area, as opposed to precision, bombing; but Harris never claimed otherwise. No critical damage to war production resulted; the thousands of fires started by the incendiaries affected mainly housing. Of the dead, 411 were civilians, and 58 service personnel, mostly members of anti-aircraft units. More than 5,000 were injured and 45,000 rendered homeless. Almost 700,000 civilians fled Cologne immediately after the raid. The psychological impact was therefore considerable. For the doomed Jews in the Warsaw ghetto news of the raid was an immense boost to morale. One diarist noted: 'As for us our death is now pre-paid.'

The basic technique involved – the use of massed squadrons in a compact and tightly controlled bomber stream – had proved itself. The arrival of a thousand aircraft in only ninety minutes had saturated the anti-aircraft defences en route and over Cologne, and thus minimised casualties among the raiders; the heavy use of incendiaries had, as intended, overwhelmed the city's fire-fighting resources. No firestorm had resulted – Cologne was largely a modern city and its streets were wide – but in a dozen similar raids on cities including Hamburg, firestorms were to prove devastating. Most importantly for Harris, his command, and the future of such raids, bomber losses were low: at 4 per cent lower than Harris had dared to hope, and less than half of what Churchill had been prepared for. Bomber Command had established itself as a weapon, however expensive and unwieldy, that would be used again and again as long as the war lasted.

Flying that night a barely serviceable aircraft of fundamentally flawed design – uncomfortable facts that go unmentioned in the official citation – Leslie Manser had, in accordance with Harris's pre-flight mass briefing, pressed home his attack to his precise objective with the utmost determination and resolution. In truth, whatever was to happen over Cologne, L7301 had left RAF Skellingthorpe with, from the start, only limited prospects of returning. It reached scarcely half the operational altitude allocated to it, and both its always-doubtful engines had failed while it was still 300 miles from base; despite this, it had fulfilled its mission and six of its seven aircrew survived the war. That they did is due entirely to the skill, self-sacrifice and courage of the seventh, its twenty-one-year-old pilot.

Sixty years later, when the area of the crash site in Belgium was being developed, efforts were made to recover any remains of the Manchester. A propeller blade in good condition was found, prompting locals to commemorate the events of the morning of 31 May 1942, and to declare that 'this propeller blade would serve as a reminder not only to the bravery of Pilot Officer Leslie Manser VC, but also to the bravery of many local and more distant people, who, at great personal risk, aided the escape of five of the six crewmembers'. On 31 June 2004 a small memorial, in which the propeller blade was incorporated, was unveiled in the presence of local dignitaries, representatives of the RAF and the Belgian air force, and close relatives of Manser, Baveystock, Barnes, King and Naylor.

Earlier in the year – on the sixtieth anniversary of Manser's death – the person who recovered the propeller blade had given a short address. It began: 'Sixty-two years ago today, an RAF twin-engined Manchester bomber met its end in Molenbeersel. Sadly, the pilot, Pilot Officer Leslie Manser, perished in the crash.' Its closing words serve to put the thousand-bomber raid on Cologne into a wider perspective: 'Today, we may take our liberty for granted. Hopefully, this memorial will serve as a reminder that at one time this was a different matter. Let us hope it helps those who follow us to recognise the true price of national liberty, personal freedom, and peace.'

Manser was one of a select band of heroes: one of only nineteen members of Bomber Command awarded the Victoria Cross, nine of them posthumously. He is buried in the Commonwealth War Graves Commission cemetery at Heverlee, in Belgium. Near him are two other posthumous VC winners: Flying Officer Garland, aged twenty-one – the first of four brothers to be killed in the war – and his observer, Sergeant Gray, aged twenty-six. Among almost a thousand headstones at Heverlee are those of 752 British airmen, 157 Canadians, 45 Australians, 17 New Zealanders, 11 Poles, one South African and one American. The American, First Lieutenant West, DFC, was a member of the United States Army Air Force, attached to the RAF. Most graves have a message inscribed on them; that on Manser's grave reads: 'He died to do his duty.'

5

Heroes amid the Holocaust

*Charles Coward, British POWs and
Jane Haining*

NORWAY

North Sea

SWEDEN

Baltic Sea

DENMARK

SOVIET UNION *since 1945*

AMERICAN ENCLAVE

BRITAIN

Danzig • Stutthof

Ravensbrück • Treblinka •

Belsen • Berlin • P O L A N D *since 1945*

BRITISH ZONE SOVIET ZONE

G E R M A N Y • Torgau

Dunkirk • Gross Rosen •

FRENCH ZONE

C Z E C H O S L O V A K I A Auschwitz • Buna-Monowitz

AMERICAN ZONE

F R A N C E

FRENCH ZONE

SWITZERLAND

A U S T R I A H U N G A R Y Budapest •

I T A L Y

Adriatic Sea

0 kilometres 300
0 miles 200

© Martin Gilbert 2008

The most vicious consequence of the Nazi domination of Europe from 1940 to 1945 was the vast programme of systematic slaughter of the millions of people herded to their deaths in squalid concentration camps, the names of which – Treblinka, Auschwitz, Bergen-Belsen and many others – are synonymous with the darkest years of European civilisation. Yet amid the sheer scale of these atrocities, and in the face of a tyranny that seemed overwhelmingly powerful, there were individuals whose humanity and courage shine out from that dreadful darkness.

In a book published in 2007, I described how Raoul Wallenberg, a daring Swedish diplomat, saved thousands of Hungarian Jews by the liberal use of official-looking documentation asserting 'Swedish connections', before he disappeared for ever, dying in Soviet captivity. Here I want to draw attention to a number of people who equalled him in their courage, and did so without the advantages – wealth, diplomatic cover, aristocratic connections – that Wallenberg deployed. They are respectively a British NCO, a 'little platoon' of ordinary British Tommies, and a former secretary from south-west Scotland who found herself – like Wallenberg – protecting Jewish people in wartime Hungary.

Charles Coward joined the British Army in 1937 at the comparatively advanced age of thirty-two. Only three years later, in the early months of the Second World War, he was a quartermaster battery sergeant major with the Royal Artillery, an appointment tradi-tionally requiring leadership, authority, and sometimes a certain rascally ingenuity in getting things done. Throughout the rest of the war, and in the most unusual circumstances, he displayed all three qualities to a remarkable degree – and managed to engineer the escape of several hundred Jews from a slave labour camp vital to German war production.

Coward was captured on 25 May 1940 during the retreat towards Dunkirk. As a prisoner of war he made numerous attempts to escape – many of which almost succeeded. As a prisoner he was troublesome in the extreme, committing acts of sabotage, and even impersonating a wounded German soldier while on the run. For these offences he was eventually sent to Stalag 8B, the camp for British POWs next to Auschwitz's vast slave labour complex at the Buna-Monowitz synthetic oil factory.

Amid the cruelties of Buna, Coward's initiative, leadership and subversive resourcefulness again came to the fore. By then quite fluent in German, and also forceful and experienced, he was appointed by his fellow British POWs as their Red Cross liaison officer, with official responsibilities for the welfare of his fellow inmates, many of whom – against the terms of the Geneva Conventions – were working as forced labourers in the adjoining IG Farben industrial complex.

This role brought with it some freedom to move around, and Coward made the most of it. As he had done in his earlier camps, he organised and supported acts of sabotage. He also observed and documented details of how trainloads of Jews and other 'enemies of the Third Reich' from all over Europe were processed and selected either for the many labour camps in the area, or for the gas chambers. He established communication with the British authorities via coded letters to a fictitious relative, and managed to pass on to them what he had seen of the day-to-day operation of what we now term 'the Holocaust'.

After the war, the testimony of 'Charles J. Coward of 133 Chichester Road, Edmonton, North London', in a long affidavit dated 24 July 1947, was presented to the international military tribunal at Nuremberg. It makes harrowing reading. In it he describes how a captured British naval officer – a ship's doctor who was Jewish – had been separated from his comrades, sent to the slave labour camp in Buna and had managed to get a note to

Coward asking that he make contact with his family in Sunderland. Coward bribed an SS guard and arranged to join a labour detail returning to that part of the prison complex where the doctor was being held. There he discovered conditions that almost defied description: two or three men in narrow wooden bunks designed for one and food so scarce that prisoners fought over it – so scarce that, as Coward explained to the tribunal: 'When the inmates were counted, the other chaps would hold up the dead for accounting purposes . . . they stood the dead men up for roll call . . . to draw their rations.'

Moved to action by the plight of the Jewish slave labourers, Coward devised an audacious and elaborate scheme to obtain non-Jewish documentation for as many of them as possible. He found an SS sergeant major, a senior camp guard with a particular liking for the chocolate supplied by the Red Cross to British POWs, and through him obtained access to the corpses and – just as importantly – to the documentation of the non-Jewish prisoners, Frenchmen, Dutchmen and Belgians among them, who had died in their section of the Buna labour camp complex.

Coward arranged for Jewish slave labourers to hide in the ditch beside the route along which those Jews who had been judged to be no longer fit for work were being marched to the gas chambers at nearby Auschwitz. He then laid the non-Jewish corpses on the road to give the impression they had died on the march. Jewish slave labourers, given non-Jewish identity documentation by Coward, thus escaped the inevitable sentence of death they faced simply for being Jewish. By such gruesome and persistent ingenuity, more than 400 Jews were saved.

Coward's report to the Sixth Military Tribunal at Nuremberg was detailed and powerful, and revealed the ruthless and frequently murderous exploitation of concentration camp prisoners in the service of German war industry. It helped secure the conviction of senior IG Farben officials for their involvement in the Buna-Monowitz slave labour complex. And in 1963 a tree was planted in Coward's honour in the Avenue of the Righteous in Yad Vashem, the Holocaust Memorial and Museum in Jerusalem, in recognition of his unique role in saving the lives of Jewish slave labourers without hope.

Coward died in 1976 at the age of seventy-one. On learning of his death, a senior Yad Vashem official wrote to his family: 'We will long remember and will pass on to posterity the memory of Mr Coward's heroic and selfless actions, which he rendered in service to his fellow man. Our sages were addressing themselves to men like Mr Coward when they taught: "He who saves one life, it is as if he had saved the entire world".'

In 2003 a blue plaque was put up on 133 Chichester Road, Edmonton, where Coward lived until his death, to commemorate the life of a courageous and truly exceptional man; one who rose to a series of remarkable challenges, and was able to save the lives of hundreds who would otherwise have become victims of the Holocaust.

In a contrasting, but no less noble, endeavour, a group of ordinary British soldiers worked together during the last months of the war in extraordinary circumstances to save the life of one young Jewish woman, Sara Matuson.

On the morning of 26 January 1945, a group of ten British prisoners of war from Stalag 20B were at work on a German farm twenty-six miles from Danzig. Three hundred inmates – women and children – on a death march from Stutthof concentration camp towards the Baltic coast were brought to a halt near them and repeatedly beaten and brutalised by their guards.

Among them was Sara Matuson: she managed to break away from the march and run into a barn, where she hid by lying in the animals' feeding trough. 'Quite a bit of time passed,' she later recalled, 'and a man came in and I asked if he was Polish . . . he said he was British.' His exact words were: 'Don't move, I'm English – don't be afraid'; her immediate thought, she remembered, was: 'English! I knew I was saved!' That soldier was Stan Wells, one of the British POWs – 'He went into the farmhouse and brought me bread.'

Bill Fisher, another of the POWs put to work on the farm – and the diarist of the group – recorded the sequel:

Stan comes to me after dinner and tells me a Jewess has got away and he has her hiding in a cow's crib. I suggest moving her to loft over camp. Plenty straw and the chimney from our fire will keep her warm. I arrange to take her to the camp. Wait till nearly dusk and go to Stan's farm, he hands over girl. I tell her to walk five paces near, on the other side of the road, and speak to no one. She is crippled, too frightened to understand me, grabs my arm.

Fisher admitted to feeling 'a bit windy' at the prospect of helping her, 'as it is a definite "crime" for prisoners to speak or walk with women'; but soon the group had managed to get 'hot water, soap, towel, old clothes, slacks, food', which they 'rushed up to her':

. . . Take all clothing off kid, give her paraffin for lice in her hair and bid her goodbye. She grabs my hand and kisses it – and tries to thank me, calls me a hero – I say roughly 'Drop it, we are comrades, only doing what we can.'

Sara Matuson recalled the care her rescuers took of her:

[Bill Fisher] brought me a full length coat and put it on top of my clothes and walked with me through the town. Luckily we weren't stopped – the guards must have thought I looked like a prisoner of war. He took me to the barn and put me upstairs and made a hole in the straw. The straw was for the horses. A couple of the men came that night – one of them a medic – and they brought stuff for my feet which had frostbite, they brought me paraffin for the lice and food, I mustn't forget the food. I was so hungry and they will tell you how much I ate.

Bill Fisher recorded in his prison diary:

Everyone brings in food for our escapee! . . . peas, ducks, hens, best part of a pig. Bread by loaves – and believe me she's ate three loaves today and five bowls of soup – somewhere around twenty-two pounds of food. She's ill now – sick diarrhoea. Suggest only milk for a few days . . .

We had a good look at her. Her eyes are large as is usual with starvation, sunken cheeks, no breasts. Hair has not been cut, body badly marked with sores caused by scratching lice bites. Head still a bit matted and lice still obviously in. I got my forefinger and thumb around the upper part of her arm easily . . . Feet blue and raw with frostbite, the right heel is eaten away from frost and constant rubbing of badly fitting clog.

'They bathed me,' Sara Matuson remembered. 'All I had was a dress with a very big red Jewish star on the back of it, a thin coat and a blanket. I was very sick.' Over the next few weeks, the POWs nursed her back to health: 'everyday I was visited with food. I only met one who would come up with food – he was Alan Edwards.'

After the first week, the British soldiers, among them Tommy Noble, a Scot, decided that their Jewish stowaway could visit them, and smuggled her into their room at the POW camp. Alan Edwards made the arrangements:

He got a sweater and coat to cover the dress shoes and stockings. I still had flannel underpants from the camp, they must have washed them for me. They pushed me through a window and I met them. We all spoke German. They then pushed me back up into the straw [in a hayloft]. They overheard that the horses were being moved away and that the straw – my home – was going. They said they would think of something – build a double wall or some-thing but that they would save me. They were all in this together.

Sara Matuson had been under the protection of the British POWs for ten weeks when Edwards visited her one evening and told her that they would be moving out under German guard that same night: 'He said that either Stan was not going with us and I would go as the extra fellow or that a Polish chap had an extra bed for me and would pick me up and keep me. The fellow never showed up. The men who saved my life were moved on – it was nearly the end of the war.'

The Stutthof death march from which Sara Matuson had escaped had started two weeks earlier with 1,200 female prisoners – among them Sara's mother and little sister, Hannah. Only three hundred were still alive by the time they reached the farm where the Stalag 20B prisoners were working.

After the British POWs were ordered westward Sara Matuson laid low in the barn until liberation, which came a few weeks later: she then made her way to a displaced persons camp in the Western Zone of Germany.

Not long after the war, Sara Matuson wrote to the Holocaust Memorial Museum in Jerusalem seeking recognition for all ten British soldiers:

If one of the ten had been against hiding me, I would not be alive today. This was truly a unanimous decision. It is not who of the prisoners of war brought me food, or tended my frostbite, or who applied paraffin to my hair, or bathed me or who nursed me back to health. All of them were involved. All had to agree; all took equal responsibility and equal risk. Had I been discovered all of us would have been shot. They had all decided, despite the danger, that they would save from the Germans that poor Jewish girl who chanced into their lives.

She also gave more details of the bravery and initiative of the ten:

In the morning when the men were led to work they would bring me food under the guise of hanging laundry in the barn. They had sawed through the bars of their own prison and in the evening sneaked up to the loft to bring me food. The police station was right outside and the danger fearful. I would certainly have been shot together with the ten prisoners of war, all of whom had families and homes in England. I had nobody, and no one would have known had I been killed. I would just have been another one of the Six Million, but they had much more to risk and it was close to going home. They could touch freedom.

Sara Matuson's thoughtful tribute to the quiet heroism of the ordinary British soldiers who risked their lives to save hers, reaches out across the years to give us a unique insight: how, amidst the Holocaust, an individual facing certain death thought and felt about her plight, and how she was saved from the savagery of the Third Reich in its last throes by the humanity, courage and common decency of a group of unassuming Tommies.

Too easily, now that more than sixty years have passed, the sheer scale of the Holocaust numbs us to its individual realities: the captivity, suffering and death of six million people, 1.5 million of them children, each with family, a history, and unique emotions and responses. But when an individual emerges as clearly as Sara Matuson does, telling her story in her own words, the modern reader is taken aback: the events of more than sixty years ago are no longer cold history. The details – of lice and sores, hunger, privation, and fear; then of food, warmth, clothing, care and survival – catch us unawares. Suddenly, the sheer horror of the Holocaust becomes personal.

Sixty years later, when Sir Martin Gilbert, the distinguished Second World War historian, was giving a lecture on the 'Righteous Gentiles' to an audience in the United States, telling them of the deeds of this group of POWs, he was astonished when a sprightly elderly lady came up to him and introduced herself as Sara Matuson. She was delighted that their courage had been thus recognised, and spoke with profound gratitude and affection for the soldiers who had saved her life.

Jane Haining, who died in Auschwitz in 1944, is only the second Scot to be commemorated as a Righteous Gentile at Yad Vashem. She was born into a farming family in the parish of Dunscore in rural southwest Scotland in 1897. When she was only five her mother died. A distant female relative moved in to look after Jane and her sister while her father ran the farm. Educated at Dumfries Academy during the First World War, Jane shone academically, but the family's circumstances meant that on leaving school she had to go straight to work. She moved to Paisley and joined the world-famous J & P Coats thread-making firm as a clerical assistant.

Although she was promoted to the post of senior secretary, a lifetime of office work did not inspire her. What did was a meeting in Glasgow describing the work of the Church of Scotland Jewish Mission. Jane turned to the friend who had accompanied her and declared: 'I have found my life's work.' For some years, as an active church member and a Sunday school teacher, she had involved herself in social causes. To prepare for her new vocation she left her job with Coats and took a diploma at the Glasgow School of Domestic Science. Shortly after she saw an advertisement in the Church of Scotland magazine *Life and Work* for the job of matron of the girls' home of the Jewish Mission in Budapest. She applied, was considered an outstanding candidate, and was appointed immediately.

After missionary training at St Colm's and having learned to speak some Hungarian – one of the most difficult of all the European languages – she took up her duties in 1932, at the age of thirty-five. These involved looking after 400 girls aged from six to sixteen, of whom around two-thirds were Jewish, and thirty to forty of them boarders. Famous for her Scottish-accented Hungarian, she was popular with what became a rising number of pupils: a mix of Christian and Jewish girls, some there simply for the good education on offer, but others – many of them orphans from broken or poverty-stricken homes – who had converted to Christianity.

It was in caring for these unwanted Jewish children that Jane Haining found her real vocation; and they found in her a devoted friend and carer. Her letters home speak of the challenges and rewards of her work: 'We have one nice little mite who is an orphan and is coming to school for the first time. She seems to be a lonely wee soul and needs lots of love. We shall see what we can do to make life a little happier for her.'

In 1939, when war broke out, Jane Haining was at home on a rare period of leave in Scotland. She immediately undertook the hazardous journey back to Budapest, but on arriving there discovered that many of her missionary colleagues were being recalled. She decided to remain at her post. With the departure of most of the mission staff, Jane was increasingly overworked. Her sister later recalled: 'She was quite determined not to come home, although all the rest of the mission did. She said she would stay with the children at the time of need.'

Twice more Jane Haining was urgently requested to return home, but she refused, saying she was needed in Budapest and would not be happy if she deserted her charges. She wrote to her sister: 'If these children need me in the days of sunshine, how much more do they need me in the days of darkness?'

Over the next four and a half years, as the tide of war swept across Europe and Hungary aligned itself with Germany, all foreign civilians were again advised to leave the country, but Jane remained, refusing to leave despite clear and growing danger.

Hungary continued to act as an ally of Germany, and as tensions rose, and Britain declared war on Hungary in December 1941, her mission school became more and more popular. Jewish families realised that the best hope for their children might be the sanctuary of the Church of Scotland. As an elderly Jew from Budapest later remembered, the mission was seen as offering refuge for Jewish girls against the threat of rape and deportation. The same witness describes visiting Jane during this period: 'Jewish parents put their girls there for an English education. As things got worse, they put them in there hoping that, being under the protection of the Scottish mission, they would escape.'

In March 1944, German troops entered Hungary. All the Scottish missionaries were ordered to leave, but Jane Haining disobeyed. She was determined to take care of her children, and remained with them. Her sister remembers that it was 'no surprise' that she refused to come back: 'She would never have had a moment's happiness if she had come home and left the children.'

The arrival of Adolf Eichmann in Hungary in March 1944, in the wake of the German Army, brought new and unimaginable darkness to Budapest. Soon he was organising the mass deportation of Jews from the rest of Hungary to Auschwitz. Jane Haining was denounced to the Nazis as a British spy, perhaps simply because of her fondness for listening to the BBC, which under the German-dominated regime was a serious crime. It is said that another factor in her eventual arrest was that she had disciplined the young son-in-law of the school cook, who was a member of the Hungarian Arrow Cross fascist party, for eating the girls' food.

Early in May 1944 two Gestapo officers knocked on Jane Haining's door. Her office and her bedroom were searched. She was given fifteen minutes to prepare for departure. One of her pupils later wrote: 'I still feel the tears in my eyes and hear in my ears the siren of the Gestapo motor car. I see the smile on her face while she bade me farewell. I never saw Miss Haining again.' Another who saw her being taken away wrote: 'The days of horror were coming, and Miss Haining protested against those who wanted to distinguish between the child of one race and the child of another. A long time later, I realised she had died for me and the others.'

Jane Haining was charged with working among Jews, a crime under Nazi law. Included in the evidence against her was a statement that she had been seen weeping while she sewed on her girls' uniforms the yellow Star of David, which would mark them out for deportation. She was also charged with listening to the BBC. Efforts to secure her release failed. Three weeks after her arrest, some of her friends arrived at the prison where she was being held, with a food parcel for her. She was not there; although she had never been put on trial she had already been taken to Auschwitz.

Jane Haining reached Auschwitz on 15 May, with thirty-one other women from Hungary. On the following day, the first train of Jewish deportees from Hungary arrived: 5,000 men, women and children from the provinces, in a train made up of fifty cattle wagons. From that night, the historian of Auschwitz, Danuta Czech, records: 'the chimneys of the crematoria began to smoke'. Jane was a witness, from its first day, of this terrible climax of the Holocaust.

In Auschwitz, Jane Haining had the number 79467

tattooed on her forearm. During her stay friends received two letters from her. One, written a few days before her death, asked for apples and bread as she was starving; and in cryptic lines, perhaps phrased to evade the censor, she wrote: 'There is not much to report from here. Here on the way to heaven are mountains, but not as beautiful or as high as ours.'

In July 1944, Jane Haining, judged by the SS overseers to be too weak to continue to work, was taken to the gas chambers.

Later that year the Church of Scotland head offices in George Street, Edinburgh, received a communication from the Nazi authorities in Germany relating to one of their missionaries: a Miss Jane Haining – a gesture of quite surreal bureaucratic propriety considering the brutality of the regime, and one that bore no relation to the facts as subsequently established. It read: 'Miss Haining, who was arrested on account of justified suspicion of espionage against Germany, died in hospital, July 17, of cachexia following intestinal catarrh [starvation].'

In May 1945, before the full details of her last weeks were known, Jane Haining's contribution was recognised in the land of her birth. A report presented to the General Assembly of the Church of Scotland said of her: 'Typical of all that is best in the Scottish tradition of missionary service, she gave the best years of her life to enhancing that tradition, and at last gave life itself.'

6

Against the Odds

Joseph Antelme and Violette Szabo

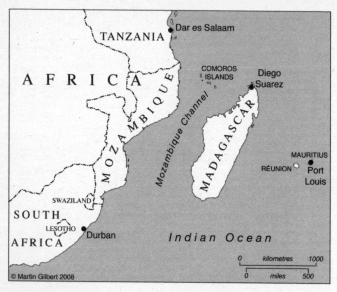

When Queen Elizabeth II unveiled the Air Forces Memorial in Runnymede to more than 20,000 Allied wartime personnel with no known grave, she said: 'Wherever and for as long as freedom flourishes on the earth, the men and women who possess it will thank them and will say they did not die in vain.'

Of all the stories of heroism in the Second World War that I came across in researching this book, those of SOE agents in France were among the most inspiring – and the most harrowing. The Special Operations Executive was formed, in Churchill's inspiring words, to 'Set Europe ablaze'. It sent its first 'F-Section' agent into occupied France in May 1941.

More than four hundred agents – around 10 per cent of them women – followed, the last going in as late as August 1944. Their motivation was clear: they hated the tyranny that had enveloped Europe. Their courage in circumstances of great and sustained danger cannot be overstated. Many failed to survive even one mission; many more, knowing the odds, went back again and again to face hazards almost unimaginable today. Their example and their sacrifice through the darkest years of the war still shine out today, and cannot fail to impress and inspire us.

At first their role was to train, support and equip emergent resistance groups to harass and sabotage the German occupation, and to make preparations for the Allied invasion. After the Normandy landings of 6 June 1944, F-Section agents, and the groups they had formed and trained, played a vital role in undermining and thwarting the German response to the arrival of the Allied armies by attacking communications and transport infrastructure, and imposing crippling delays on troop movements. Throughout, agents faced appalling risks and daunting odds. Betrayal, capture, imprisonment, torture and death were all too frequent.

The SOE agents wore no uniforms during their time in France and so had no protection from the Geneva Conventions. From the moment they landed they were vulnerable – they could be stopped and interrogated at roadblocks, betrayed by hostile locals, or find that the circuit they had come to support had been infiltrated by the Gestapo and its sympathisers. The average survival of a wireless operator in the field was only six weeks; at least a quarter of all agents failed to return. Ninety-one men and thirteen women from F Section are known to have met their deaths, the majority in concentration camps in Germany. A memorial at Valençay, near Tours, unveiled in 1991, on the fiftieth anniversary of the landing of the first agent, commemorates their sacrifice. Among the names inscribed upon it are those of Joseph Antelme ('Antelme, Major J. A. F., General List); and Violette Szabo ('Szabo, Ensign V. R. E., Women's Transport Service').

Joseph Antoine France Antelme's SOE file was released to the Public Record Office (now the National Archives) only in 2003. Even among the hundreds of daring and resolute F-Section agents, he stands out. The OBE he was awarded for his actions might now be seen as only a modest recognition of what was a very distinguished SOE career.

Antelme was born in 1900 in Port Louis in Mauritius to British parents. His family was part of the influential elite of planters and politicians – the island's so-called 'grand blancs'. After schooling at the Royal College in Port Louis, he embarked on a colourful business career as a trader and broker, ranging across the Indian Ocean from Mauritius to Madagascar, from South Africa to Réunion. By the early 1930s he had settled in Durban, as Madagascar's trade representative in South Africa.

In 1941, while serving with the South African artillery, he was recruited by SOE to join its Todd mission, led by Lieutenant-Colonel J. E. S. Todd, and was active in the mission's work in the run-up to Operation

Ironclad, the invasion of Madagascar. In February 1942 Antelme was landed on Madagascar to carry out clandestine reconnaissance, using his many contacts there to acquire valuable political and military intelligence prior to the successful British landings at Diego Suarez that May.

Antelme had already established himself as a cool and resourceful operator and in mid-1942 was transferred from Todd's HQ in Dar es Salaam to England. At SOE's Baker Street offices in London he was assigned to F Section, and sent for training: first to Beaulieu in Hampshire, later to Arisaig in Argyll. Though by then over forty, and speaking with a marked Mauritian accent, Antelme was seen as a recruit with real potential. Notes from his file describe him as 'very keen and anxious to learn', and possessing understanding and knowledge that was 'most thorough and painstaking'. In these notes, Antelme was also described as 'one of the soundest men on the course' with 'plenty of courage and completely reliable . . . one of the best types I have ever met'. In a particularly prescient comment an observer noted: 'It would take a lot to upset him once he got started and it would take a bullet to stop him.'

Antelme's first mission to France began in November 1942. The main aim of his Bricklayer network was to prepare for the Normandy landings by building resistance groups that would eventually supply the vast amounts of fresh provisions needed by the Allied forces. The aircraft carrying him encountered anti-aircraft fire over Tours, but soon afterwards he heard the order 'Action Stations' and parachuted out into the night. A reception committee met him as arranged, and conducted him to a safe house. Then his work began. In the city of Tours, as he reported on his return, there was much enemy activity: 'Troops galore on and around the station as well as in town, with members of the Feldgendarmerie in twos on their beat all over the place.'

Antelme's next stop, Poitiers, was equally dangerous. There he made a potentially fatal error – signing in at a hotel with his own signature, not that of his cover name – but managed to retrieve the situation by persuading the clerk to let him sign in afresh. He later said he learned a lot from that mistake; and soon found out just how risky the life of an F-Section agent could be. In addition to organising a new circuit as he had been instructed, he took on the much more dangerous task of rebuilding another circuit that had been compromised because its leader's identity had been uncovered. In messages back to SOE he repeatedly emphasised the importance of secrecy, 'as there have been some unfortunate leakages with fatal consequences'.

At the end of his first mission he was brought home – itself a hazardous matter involving clandestine landing strips, night landings and take-offs, and the ever-present risk of discovery – and reported on his work: two Bricklayer circuits, based at Le Mans and Troyes, established, with safe houses that allowed agents to move around without detection; preliminary work on the logistics of food supplies; and the recruitment of an agent who later proved, like Antelme himself, to be highly successful.

In May 1943, after two months in England spent debriefing and training, Antelme was again parachuted into France. But as SOE stepped up its activities, so the Gestapo expanded its countermeasures: surveillance and intelligence work, including wireless monitoring, increased; SOE circuits were successfully infiltrated using double agents recruited from among collaborationist Frenchmen. For agents like Antelme, already well known within the networks, second and third missions brought far greater risk of exposure.

Within a month a fellow agent had been arrested as a result of the activities of a Gestapo double agent. Further arrests followed. As his work took him closer to the increasingly insecure Prosper network, Antelme was in grave danger. When two Canadian agents parachuting in to join the circuit were arrested on landing, it was clear that Prosper had been smashed. Antelme immediately sought to limit the damage and sent urgent messages to his fellow agents urging them to flee before the Germans could round them up. He, meanwhile, chose to stay, hoping to gain time in which to warn colleagues in the Poitiers area, where he had operated on his previous mission.

For the Gestapo, success followed success, as the cycle of arrests, information and more arrests was repeated. As his last act of his second mission Antelme called a meeting of resistance leaders, explained the position following the collapse of Prosper, then returned to England to report to SOE on the disaster. He was also able to report on progress: despite the destruction of Prosper the build-up of food-supply logistics for the Allied armies had been sustained. 'There is not the slightest doubt,' his report concluded, 'that the food situation in France would easily provide for the feeding of an invading army of, say, 500,000 men, without the slightest prejudice caused to the civilian population . . . It must be borne in mind that it has meant considerable work and risk' – that last phrase surely qualifying as a substantial understatement. In January 1944 Antelme was awarded an OBE, though no details were made public at the time in order to protect him and his fellow agents for even more important work still to come.

By the beginning of 1944 preparations on both sides of the Channel for the Normandy landings had intensified. In France the matter of food-supply chains and the plans for the disruption of German road and rail communications became more urgent. On 29 February, Antelme, an experienced agent of proven effectiveness, was despatched again. The next note on his file reads simply: 'Did not return.'

The agent who should have met Antelme as he parachuted in had been arrested and turned, and seems to have given the Gestapo details of the time and place of Antelme's landing. Instead of being met by members of the resistance and ushered to a safe house, Antelme was arrested. Jailed first in Paris, he was subsequently taken to the concentration camp at Gross Rosen in Silesia. He was killed there on 29 March 1945.

Violette Reine Elizabeth Szabo was only twenty-two, and already a widow and a mother, when she was recruited to SOE in 1943. She was born Violette Bushel, the daughter of a British father and a French mother, and brought up in London. She was still a teenager when a chance meeting with a French soldier, Lieutenant Etienne Szabo, who had fought in the Norway campaign of 1940, led to a family meal, romance and marriage. They had a mere two weeks together as husband and wife before he set off with his regiment once more. She never saw him again. He was killed on 24 October 1942, fighting with the Free French forces in the battle of El Alamein.

Young, widowed, and facing a difficult future as a single parent, Violette Szabo – like many other war widows – was stricken by grief, and variously angry and depressed. When, a few months after her bereavement, she received an official letter from a 'Mr E. Potter' asking for a meeting about matters related to the war, she thought at first it might be something to do with her widow's pension.

It was not. It was the first, and sometimes only, stage of the SOE's recruitment process, which was by invitation only, and based on an informal interview that would, if the interviewee seemed unsuitable, be the end of the matter. However, it was made clear to possible recruits that subsequent participation depended on their free and informed choice. 'Mr E. Potter' was actually Captain Selwyn Jackson, SOE's chief recruiting officer, who would tell prospective agents to go away and sleep on the idea, saying something like: 'We'd both like to think about it. I don't want you to make up your mind too easily; it's a difficult decision to make; it's a life and death decision for both of us. I have to decide whether I can risk your life and you have to decide whether you're willing to risk it.' In his view every prospective agent had to make up his or her mind, alone, to volunteer – or not.

Violette Szabo volunteered, and by July 1943 was in training. She was the subject of mixed reports. Her

SOE files record the views of one instructor who thought her 'a physically tough self-willed girl; with plenty of confidence in herself . . . not easily rattled . . . she could probably do a useful job possibly as a courier'. Another considered her to have been 'proven to possess certain qualities which I never would have suspected of her', adding: 'She is rather a puzzle.'

At least one official concluded it was wrong for Violette Szabo to go forward as a special agent: 'After a certain amount of doubt, especially at the beginning of the course, I have come to the conclusion that this student is temperamentally unsuitable for this work . . . it is very regrettable to have to come to such a decision when dealing with a student of this type, who during the whole course has set an example to the whole party by her cheerfulness and eagerness to please.' Fortunately, this view did not prevail.

Despite these doubts, which could have ended her SOE career before it had truly begun, Szabo completed her training and was parachuted into France in April 1944. Her mission was to establish whether or not an SOE circuit had been infiltrated. She quickly reported back that it no longer existed: its members had been dispersed, and most of them arrested and deported to Germany. She survived retrieval from a clandestine landing-strip, and a trip home that included the aircraft coming under fire and shaking violently. Unable to communicate with the pilot, she assumed when they eventually reached England that they had actually crash-landed in France.

A note in Szabo's file reads: 'Just returned from an important mission in the field which she has performed admirably. It is desired to recognise this before she goes out again by commissioning her as an Ensign.' Thus it was, as a junior officer and nominally a member of the Women's Transport Service, that Szabo undertook her second mission to France in June 1944, this time as courier to SOE agent Philippe Liewer, who was in charge of coordinating networks in a resistance uprising as the Allied invasion of northwest Europe proceeded and the liberation of German-occupied France un-folded.

In the wake of the Normandy landings the Germans mobilised against the Allied forces, their levels of activity in northern France making life even more dangerous for SOE's F Section. Szabo was twice arrested by the German security services, but twice managed to get away. Random roadblocks appeared with increasing frequency, and as Szabo's car approached one of them, near the village of Salon, the driver prudently stopped 50 yards away. All three occupants got out and fled across a wheat field to the cover of a wood. Reaching a house in the wood, Szabo, in the words of her citation, 'seized a Sten-gun and as much ammunition as she could carry, barricaded herself in part of the house, and, exchanging shot for shot with the enemy, killed or wounded several of them. By constant movement she avoided being cornered, and fought until she dropped exhausted.'

Thus it was that, just as Europe was on the brink of liberation, Violette Szabo lost her own freedom; and just months before the war's end, she would lose her life. Her SOE file is full of contradictory accounts of what happened to her in the final months of her life, but the stories and recollections repeated from the men and women who came across her after her arrest tell of a woman whose spirit rose, again and again, from the misery and horror of captivity in concentration camps as the war drew to an end.

For months Violette's parents had no idea of her fate. They did not even know the type of work she had been called to do during the war, but in March 1946 they received a letter, a copy of which is in the SOE files. It began: 'It is with the greatest regret that I write to inform you that we have now received conclusive proof that Violette Szabo met her death in Ravensbruck concentration camp between the dates of January 25/February 15, 1945.' The letter included some information about what had happened to her between her arrest and her eventual death.

Szabo had spent two months in summer late 1944 in Fresnes prison in Paris, and later that year was seen in

Torgau camp, on the Elbe, where she was working in a factory, apparently in good health and spirits, and planning to escape; but by January 1945 she was in solitary confinement in Ravensbruck concentration camp, from which she never emerged. Testimony, from a witness later arrested, about her execution along with two other women, describes how the 'bearing of the three women was of the highest order and greatly impressed all those who performed and who were present at the execution'.

The letter announcing her death concluded: 'In giving this news to you, news which I know must be very difficult to bear, I should like to offer on behalf of this branch, my own very sincere sympathy. You must be very proud of the way your daughter maintained her calm dignified courage throughout her ordeal. It is testimony to that courage that she impressed and moved even those who were responsible for her death.'

Violette Szabo was only twenty-four when she died. She had served with SOE for two years. Looking back, it is clear that her courage and her sacrifice have long transcended the squalor and brutality of her captivity and death. She was posthumously awarded the Croix de Guerre and the George Cross, and her name is inscribed on the Brookwood Memorial outside London. The story of her courage lives on, a vital part of the history of SOE in which she served.

'Was it all worthwhile?' one surviving agent asked. 'What difference did it all make in the end?' But the SOE historian Professor M. R. D. Foot, himself a former wartime intelligence officer who worked with the French resistance, wrote: 'SOE provided resisters with backbone, with steely support to uphold the good cause against the bad . . . any attempt to draw up a formal profit-and-loss account would be arid indeed.'

For me, more than sixty years on, the real legacy of SOE is one of daunting and exemplary courage in a struggle against tyranny – a legacy as relevant today as it was in the darkest days of the Second World War.

7

D-Day Heroes

SAS Paratroopers and Stanley Hollis

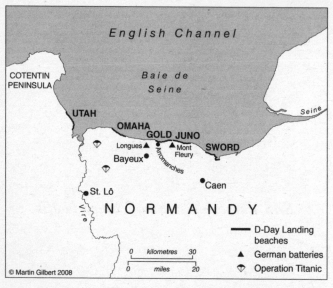

English Channel

COTENTIN
PENINSULA

*Baie de
Seine*

Seine

UTAH

OMAHA

GOLD JUNO

Longues ▲ ▲ Mont
Fleury

SWORD

Arromanches

Bayeux ●

Vire

St. Lô ●

Caen ●

N O R M A N D Y

━━━ D-Day Landing
beaches

▲ German batteries

◈ Operation Titanic

| 0 | kilometres | 30 |
| 0 | miles | 20 |

© Martin Gilbert 2008

| 0 | kilometres | 500 |
| 0 | miles | 300 |

ITALY

Adriatic Sea

BALKANS

Black Sea

GREECE

Aegean Sea

TURKEY

SICILY

Catania ●

Tunis ●

Mediterranean Sea

CYPRUS

PALESTINE

IRAQ

Western Desert

El Alamein ● Cairo ●

NORTH AFRICA

E G Y P T

Nile

Red Sea

© Martin Gilbert 2008

Operation Neptune, the assault phase of the invasion of northwest Europe that began with the Normandy landings at dawn on 6 June 1944, was the largest amphibious operation in the history of warfare. More than 130,000 troops went ashore on D-Day, alone. Supported by a huge naval bombardment and thousands of bomber and fighter-bomber aircraft, Allied forces managed to breach Rommel's strongly fortified Atlantic Wall and establish – over a series of bloody encounters and despite some grim setbacks – a foothold in northern Europe. It was the beginning of a campaign that would culminate in the German surrender at Luneburg Heath at 5.30 a.m. on 4 May 1945.

Although the Allied offensive had long been expected, initial responses from the defending forces were uncertain. For a few crucial weeks the German Army's tactical and strategic responses were influenced by the conviction that these landings were not the long-awaited invasion, but a sideshow laid on to draw their forces away from a far more powerful assault: one which the best intelligence available to them indicated would take place more than 200 miles to the northeast, in the Pas-de-Calais region, the closest point of German-occupied Europe to Britain. There, they believed, a far larger force would later cross the Channel, having used the Normandy landings as a feint to wrong-foot them and disperse and deplete their main reserves.

The commanders charged by Hitler with the defence of the coasts of German-occupied Europe therefore interpreted activities on the five landing beaches – Sword, Juno, Gold, Omaha and Utah – accordingly. This was not, however, a sideshow; this was the main event. The perceived threat to Pas-de-Calais was the product of a brilliant strategy of deception, as was the creation of false intelligence pointing to an Allied invasion of Norway, and carefully planted impressions that the continuing bomber offensive against the German industrial heartland was the Allies' main strategy in bringing about Germany's defeat.

The Allies' deception plans had evolved in great detail alongside the planning for what was in fact intended: Operation Neptune, the initial assault phase, and Overlord – the liberation of northwest Europe. 'In wartime,' Churchill had declared, 'truth is so precious that she should always be attended by a bodyguard of lies.' So, with the help of German agents who had landed in Britain and been turned, and making full use of the unique and equally well-kept secret of Enigma – the code-breaking triumph that sometimes allowed staff at Bletchley Park to read some top-secret German signals even before their intended recipients – a vast and astonishingly successful web of deceit shrouded Allied intentions and misled and misdirected the enemy. As D-Day drew near, the imperative to deceive became ever more important, and the details of that deception even more intricate.

Of all the deception operations undertaken in the run-up to the Normandy landings, Operation Titanic was one of the last. It took place on 6 June just hours before the first of the parachute and glider landings, which went in at 'H-Hour', 06.30. It stands out as one of the most ingenious deceptions of the war; it proved to be crucially effective, and sadly, among the most costly. Its name might have implied that it was a vast enterprise; it was not, though it might have appeared as such to the German defenders who witnessed it. Only ten men – two officers, two NCOs, and six troopers – all drawn from 2nd Special Air Service Regiment, took part in it. Of them, only two returned.

In May 1944, a twenty-four-year-old intelligence officer with the Special Air Services Brigade, Captain M. R. D. Foot, based at its tactical headquarters at Moor Park, near Rickmansworth, north of London, took a telephone call about an as-yet-unnamed operation that would soon take place. Foot, who had already been active with SOE choosing the areas in France where German reinforcements to Normandy could most effectively be harried by the French resistance under SOE guidance, and who would later – as Professor M. R. D. Foot – become SOE's historian, looked in his safe. From the two remaining unallocated codenames, he chose the name Titanic.

Foot was then instructed to assemble for the operation two SAS parties of five men each, and arrange to rendezvous with them at RAF Tempsford, in Bedfordshire, at 1700 hours on 'D-Day minus two'. Although Foot had been told to ask no questions about the operation, he was for practical reasons forced at that point to ask 'D-Day minus two for which operation?' The reply was 'Neptune, of course.' Foot cleared it with his commanding officer, Brigadier McLeod, and went about finding the men needed for Titanic. He approached Lieutenant-Colonel 'Paddy' Mayne, commanding officer of 1st SAS Regiment, who declined to co-operate.

Foot then approached 2nd SAS, and was met with a more positive response: though the men concerned were said to be very alarmed by the briefing for the operation, they followed their orders to the letter. The ten, all airborne-trained and experienced, were given the task of simulating mass paratroop landings in occupied France in the first hours of D-Day, at locations chosen to cause maximum distraction to the defending German forces as the landings began, and to draw them away from the real liberating forces when these were at their most vulnerable.

At the heart of the deception operation were 'Ruperts', the nickname given to the artificial paratroopers, 500 of which were to be dropped with the SAS parties. These were roughly life-size dummies, crude representations of paratroopers with trunk and limbs formed of coarse fabric stuffed with straw and sand. To confuse the enemy, and to prolong the deception, each was equipped with a self-destruct mechanism which exploded after landing and ignited 'Rupert', so leaving little immediate evidence of his true nature. Other measures intended to maximise the impact of Titanic included rifle fire played on gramophone records and amplified, and fireworks to simulate battle noise. Managing these sound effects would form the major part of the work of ten SAS men in the last hours before the D-Day landings, as the clock ticked towards the carefully coordinated landing times of the liberating forces.

The SAS teams allocated to Titanic, with their hundreds of accompanying decoys, took off late into the evening of 5 June in an airborne force consisting of Hudsons, Halifaxes and Stirlings, numbering forty in all. At 0011 hours on the 6th, Lieutenant Noel Poole,

SAS, leading a team of three, became the first man to drop into Normandy, five miles west of St Lô on the Cotentin peninsula. A few minutes later Lieutenant Harry 'Chicken' Fowles and his team landed nearby. To the east, at Isigny, near the mouth of the River Vire on the south side of the Cotentin peninsula, and only ten miles from Omaha Beach, further Titanic team members landed in woodland, accompanied by scores of fake airborne invaders. The Verey lights used to illuminate the 'dropping zone', the parachutes and the battle noises, together with the long-bottled-up tension affecting the defending forces along Rommel's Atlantic Wall, combined to good effect.

At 3 a.m., three and a half hours before the Omaha landings, a local German unit reacted to what it took to be a significant attack and attempted to report it to the general in overall charge. That officer was absent: ironically, he was attending a conference on how best to repel aerial attacks. His chief of staff, whom he had left in charge, ordered an immediate counterattack, in his words 'to counter an airborne threat', and committed to it a substantial force of between 2,000 and 3,000 men.

The 915th Infantry Regiment was the main reserve for the German division holding the sector that included Omaha Beach, where more than 34,000 men and 3,300 vehicles of the US 1st and 29th Infantry Divisions were due to land in a matter of hours. Shortly after

3.00 a.m. it was sent eastwards, across the peninsula and away from Omaha, to deal with the reported 'airborne threat'. Its troops spent many hours in woodland searching for non-existing paratroopers and even 'exchanging fire' with them.

'Bloody Omaha' that morning proved to be a hotly contested landing, in which the liberating Allied forces sustained heavy casualties and struggled to gain a foothold; and from which General Omar Bradley, in command of the entire US 1st Army, considered at one point the possibility of evacuation. For the defending German forces, the absence of 915th Regiment, its only reserve brigade, might have made a crucial difference. Professor Foot, as one who participated in the planning of Operation Titanic, certainly thinks so: these men, he claims, would otherwise have been used 'to drive Bradley back into the sea'.

Of the ten men who took off from RAF Tempsford for Operation Titanic, only two returned home, having found safety behind the front line as the Allies advanced. Of the remainder, it is thought that two died in battle and the rest were captured, later dying or being killed in concentration camps.

For the SAS it was a harrowing encounter, and a dark, if brief, chapter in its history. As Professor Foot has written: 'Titanic is remembered as a disaster, for a sound regimental reason – of the ten men who went on it, only two came back.' But the valour and sacrifice of these ten courageous men were crucial for the fate of the American infantrymen who, in their thousands, fought against the odds to storm the beach twenty miles to the north: Bradley and his men were not driven back into the sea.

Out of all the soldiers involved in the Normandy landings, just one, Company Sergeant Major Stanley Hollis of the Green Howards, was awarded the VC. His story is one of extraordinary courage and outstanding service in the ranks. Landing with D Company, 6th Green Howards, on Gold Beach, he demonstrated again and again courage and leadership of the highest order; triumphing, by his own heroism and by his example to others, in a truly remarkable series of classic infantry encounters, as men of his regiment first landed, then crossed the beach, and then fought their way inland to secure crucial territory and establish a bridge-head in Normandy in the crucial hours of the morning of 6 June.

Stanley Hollis was born in Loftus on Teesside in 1912. A bright and rebellious boy, he won a scholarship to a grammar school in Redcar but could not take it up because his parents couldn't afford the cost of the uniform; they needed him to work in the family fish shop. At seventeen he joined the Merchant Navy, leaving after a serious bout of malaria contracted in West Africa. Unemployment and irregular work on farms and as a lorry driver saw him through the hard times of the late 1920s and the '30s, and in 1939 he joined the local infantry regiment, the Green Howards, as a territorial, in order to serve with his friends and – as he freely admitted – for a regular income.

Early in his service he applied in vain for a transfer to the Royal Navy, then for a commission with the Army – which was denied because of his lack of education. But his potential as a soldier was soon recognised by his regiment, with which he served throughout the war. His loyalty to the Green Howards, and his capacity to inspire his fellow soldiers within it to even greater achievements, are a tribute both to his personal qualities and to the British regimental system. When asked what inspired his greatest feats on the first day of the Normandy landings he would answer quietly: 'Because I was a Green Howard.'

In an archive recording held in the regimental museum in Richmond, Yorkshire, Hollis explains: 'Well, you must understand I come from Middlesbrough, where everybody is connected with the Green Howards in some way or other . . . and, of course, the Green Howards are the be all and the end all of the British Army, and I was proud to be a Green Howard. The best moment of my life was when I was made a Sergeant Major.'

Hollis first saw active service as a despatch rider in France in 1940, and was wounded in the retreat to Dunkirk. Promoted to sergeant on his return to England, he was sent to the Middle East, serving in Iraq, Palestine and Cyprus. In 1942 his battalion joined the North African campaign as part of the 50th Northumbrian Division which, under Montgomery, fought from El Alamein to Tunis. Following victory in the Western Desert, the division took part in the 1943 invasion of Sicily, where Hollis, who had just been promoted CSM, was wounded in the battle for Primasole Bridge near Catania and recommended for – but not awarded – the Distinguished Conduct Medal.

Montgomery thought highly of the by-then battle-hardened 50th Division, allocating to it the 'dangerous honour' of forming the first wave to land on Gold Beach on 6 June 1944. Its task was first to carry out an opposed landing on the heavily defended Normandy coast, then to advance inland, cut the Bayeux to Caen road, secure the port of Arromanches and take out a key German gun emplacement at Longues. In Hollis' own words, recorded in 1947 on location on the Normandy battlefields:

We did our training for the invasion up at Inverary in Scotland. We knew exactly how to do it and what to do. We had done it once before in Sicily, but this was very good additional training. It was miserable. It was January and February and cold. However, we got over it and we came down to the south coast to prepare for the invasion . . . We were shown aerial photographs – yards and yards of them – of the whole beach area that concerned us. Quite clearly shown up were our objectives . . . We had a very good picture of what we were going to do when we got here.

Training and accumulated combat experience can account for some of what followed, but only high courage and selfless leadership can fully explain the sequence of events that resulted in Hollis being awarded the only D-Day VC. After more than an hour in landing craft on rough seas, D Company, 6th Green Howards, lost some men by drowning, with others killed and wounded by enemy fire as they reached the shore. Under heavy fire from the German defending forces, and with a minefield to negotiate, Hollis led a small detachment in a dash from the surf, along the beach, then straight up to the high-water mark, to lay down a smokescreen and rake with Bren-gun fire the hedge in which the enemy was concealed.

Hollis then took part in an advance across the minefield by two platoons, both of which sustained casualties from small-arms fire from a concealed enemy position that was able to fire into the rear of the advancing troops. As Hollis and his men gained some height the officer in charge, Major Lofthouse, spotted, only 20 yards away, the source of the firing.

'There is a pillbox there, Sergeant Major,' the major said. It was an observation, not an order – because none was necessary. Hollis charged the pillbox alone, firing his Sten gun and drawing machine-gun fire, but closing in regardless. He then climbed on top of the structure, leaned over and dropped a grenade through a firing-slit. Entering the pillbox from the rear he found two Germans, dead, and 'quite a lot of prisoners . . . quite willing to forget all about the war'.

The large number of prisoners – about twenty – was subsequently explained by the discovery that this and the neighbouring pillbox, which also surrendered to Hollis, had been the command post for an important German gun emplacement, the Mont Fleury battery, into which Hollis and his men proceeded to advance. From its heights the beaches were clearly visible; Hollis reflected later that until then he 'had been firmly convinced that the Green Howards were the only people fighting this bloody war', and only at that point realised the vast scale of the landings that had followed the first wave.

By the afternoon there were new challenges, two miles inland, as Hollis led a platoon to check and clear farmhouses and a village on the road; he again came under fire. He immediately ordered a section attack with Bren-gun fire to engage its presumed source. Within moments seven or eight of his men fell dead. Hollis consulted with his company commander, then led a party of three, armed with Bren guns and an anti-tank gun, to take on a strongpoint, a hundred yards away, consisting of a well-concealed field-gun crew armed also with machine guns. When he was only 50 yards away he exchanged fire with a sniper, sustaining a bullet graze on his cheek. Outgunned, the attack stalled. Hollis then risked his life providing covering fire, telling his commanding officer: 'I took them in there, I will try to get them out.' Two of his men had stayed behind as Hollis and the others had been forced to withdraw. Advancing alone towards the enemy position, Hollis, firing his Bren gun, was able to distract the Germans as the two got safely back.

The *London Gazette* of 17 August 1944 carried the announcement of the award of the VC to 4390973 WO II Stanley Hollis for bravery in Normandy on 6 June 1944. Hollis had sustained a leg wound in further fighting in September 1944 and was evacuated to England that month, and was able to attend an investiture on 10 October 1944, where he was duly decorated by George VI at Buckingham Palace. The last paragraph of the citation read: 'Wherever fighting was heaviest,

C.S.M. Hollis appeared and, in the course of a magnificent day's work, he displayed the utmost gallantry and on two separate occasions his courage and initiative prevented the enemy from holding up the advance at critical stages. It was largely through his heroism and resource that the Company's objectives were gained and casualties were not heavier, and by his own bravery he saved the lives of many of his men.'

Hollis was a large and fit man: a muscular 6 foot 2, with fiery red hair and huge hands. As a soldier he was brave, even heroically so; but he was no angel, and from time to time, for various reasons during his army career, he was demoted from sergeant to corporal, then promoted back again. He was modest about his achievements: 'What I did was nothing to do with courage. I just got mad at seeing my mates go down around me.' He had a gentle and ironic sense of humour too, claiming: 'The bravest thing I ever did was to allow an Army dentist to pull out one of my teeth.'

Although a legend in his regiment, according to his fellow Green Howard, Field Marshal Lord Inge, Hollis – one of forty-eight Yorkshiremen to have won the VC in its history – did not settle in time of peace. In the post-war years he was variously a sandblaster, a partner in a motor-repair business, and a marine engineer; he then managed pubs from 1955 until his death in 1972.

Ten years later his medals were auctioned by Sotheby's for a record £32,000. They were subsequently presented by their owner to the Green Howards regimental museum, where they can be seen today.

8

The Bravest of Brothers

Derek and Hugh Seagrim

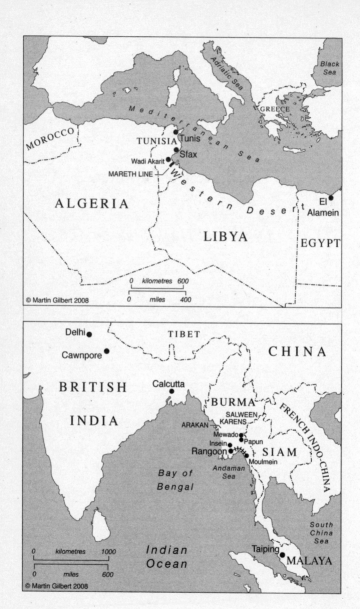

Near St Mary's church in the small village of Whissonsett in Norfolk stands a memorial to two brothers, both of whom were killed in the Second World War. It is engraved with images of the Victoria Cross and the George Cross. Derek Seagrim VC and his youngest brother Hugh Seagrim GC are the only two brothers to hold the VC and the GC respectively. They were the sons of a local clergyman, the Reverend Charles Seagrim, rector of the parish of Whissonsett-with-Horningtoft.

Even by the tolerant standards of the rural clergy in the early twentieth century, the Seagrim family was unusual, if not slightly eccentric. Charles Seagrim arrived in his Norfolk parish in 1909 at the age of forty-seven having served as a missionary in South Africa. Villagers recall a dutiful, though fragile of health, rector, his kindly wife, their large and lively family of boys and a Great Dane (with attendant dog-cart, made by the rector and used for collecting hedgerow vegetation to feed his rabbits). The second youngest son, Jack, recalled that they 'were as poor as church mice', but, thanks to their parents' cheerful commitment to the welfare of all the villagers and their generosity with what they had, the boys enjoyed a lively if not an affluent upbringing.

They mixed freely with the local children (who would ride in the dog-cart, sometimes at alarming speeds); and their home, a vast rectory with a sprawling garden, became a focal point for the community. In the absence of any village playing fields its lawns were made available for cricket matches and football. The gardens accommodated fetes, garden parties and horticultural shows, and if the weather turned bad such events might simply be invited to move indoors to take over the whole ground floor of the rectory.

The Seagrim boys went around barefoot most of the year, did not attend the village school, and had no formal education until they were old enough to go off to boarding school in Norwich. One villager recalled: 'While we sat there doing our lessons . . . they were running from the rectory, past the school and around the churchyard with the dogs. They were always climbing up the trees at the rectory and jumping out. They didn't seem to be scared of anything.' By the time their father died in the late 1920s, four of the five boys had joined the armed forces. All were to see active service in the Second World War.

The third oldest brother, Lieutenant-Colonel Derek Seagrim, earned his VC for leading his battalion of Green Howards in an assault on a strongpoint in the Mareth Line in North Africa on 21 and 22 March 1943. He died soon afterwards of wounds sustained at Wadi Akarit. He was forty years old. His youngest brother, Major Hugh Seagrim, GC DSO MBE, served for two years behind enemy lines in Burma, in circumstances of appalling hardship, uncertainty and danger. He died in Rangoon in September 1943, aged just thirty-four.

Derek Seagrim was born in 1903 and attended King Edward VI School in Norwich, where many years before Horatio Nelson, also the son of a Norfolk clergyman, had been a pupil. He was commissioned into the Green Howards in 1923, served in Jamaica, Palestine and China, and was then seconded for three years to East Africa with the King's African Rifles. He rejoined 1st Battalion, the Green Howards, in Palestine in 1939 as an intelligence officer, and served on the staff during the Greek campaign of 1941. In October 1942 he was back with the Green Howards, leading 7th Battalion as an acting lieutenant-colonel during General Montgomery and Eighth Army's first great victory, the Battle of El Alamein, a turning point in the Desert War.

From then the Allies were on the offensive in North Africa. By the spring of 1943 Eighth Army had driven Rommel hundreds of miles back across the Western

Desert, as far as Tunisia. The once invincible Afrika-korp – minus its Commander-in-Chief, General Erwin Rommel, who had departed permanently for Europe – was then under Italian command; and the combined Axis forces were caught between Montgomery's westward advance and strong British and American forces that had landed in Morocco and Algeria in November 1942 and were pushing east. The Mareth Line – a prewar French fortification in southern Tunisia, at a point where the mountains are 30 miles from the Mediterranean – offered the retreating Germans and Italians at least a chance to hold off Eighth Army, although Rommel had advised against it before leaving, preferring a stronger position further to the west.

Operation Pugilist, Montgomery's attack on the Mareth Line, began on 19 March 1943, and did not go well. The 50th (Northumbrian) Infantry Division, which included the 7th Green Howards, eventually succeeded in breaking through the Italian front line; but difficult terrain and foul weather impeded tank and artillery support, and a powerful counterattack by the 15th Panzer Division three days later largely succeeded. Three days of fierce and costly fighting had changed little.

On 20 March, in the midst of that battle, the 7th Green Howards came under heavy fire while attacking a well-defended enemy position. When it seemed that continuing enemy fire would be overwhelming, and that the attack might fail, Derek Seagrim took the initiative and led his troops forward. An anti-tank ditch blocked their path. Seagrim helped to position a scaling ladder and was the first to go across. He and his men were then confronted by two enemy machine-gun posts. Seagrim led an attack on the posts, he and his men putting both out of action and killing twenty of the defenders. The battalion dug in to await the inevitable counterattack, which came the following day. With his men in defence, Seagrim encouraged and directed them fearlessly, running repeatedly, under heavy fire, from position to position until the enemy fell back. For these actions he was recommended for the Victoria Cross.

The direct attack on the Mareth Line had stalled. The Axis defences remained viable if not intact; but on 26 March a powerful Allied outflanking manoeuvre followed. Using a route inland of the landward end of the Mareth Line, a route considered impassable by a modern force, Eighth Army infantry units, followed by an armoured brigade, succeeded in outflanking the Mareth defences, which were abandoned by the 28th. Caught between Montgomery's advance and the combined US and British forces to their rear, the Axis forces retreated, digging in forty miles to the northwest at Wadi Akarit.

The battle at Wadi Akarit, the last major armoured and infantry encounter of the war in the Western

Desert, ended with victory for the Allies on 6 April. The broken Axis forces fell back towards their main supply base of Tunis, and a final Eighth Army assault by IX Corps broke through its defences on 6 May. The remaining Italian and German units – almost 300,000 men – surrendered on the 12th. The war in North Africa was over.

The following day, 13 May 1943, the *London Gazette* carried the announcement of the award of the VC to Lieutenant-Colonel Derek Anthony Seagrim, of 7th Battalion, the Green Howards. It was a posthumous award. Severely wounded in the battle of Wadi Akarit, Derek had died in a military hospital at nearby Sfax on 6 April.

Hugh Seagrim's story is very different but no less heroic. It is one of high courage and leadership through the dark years of the war in the Far East. Always short of weapons, ammunition and supplies, and only rarely in touch with higher command, he raised and led a local force of Karen Levies. He remained with the Karens throughout the occupation, threatening and harassing Japanese lines of communication, and maintaining, however precariously, a British presence between the invasion of Burma and the arrival of Slim's Fourteenth Army.

Born in 1909, Hugh Seagrim was the youngest of the

five Seagrim boys. He too attended King Edward VI School in Norwich. In 1927, when he was in his last year in school, his father died. Plans for university and a career in medicine were now unaffordable. An application for Dartmouth and the Royal Navy failed – he was partially colour-blind – but an application for Sandhurst succeeded, and he followed his brothers into the army.

Like many a young officer of limited means, Hugh Seagrim opted for service with the Indian Army. After a one-year attachment to the Highland Light Infantry in Cawnpore he applied to join the Burma Rifles and was posted to the Malayan town of Taiping, joining the regiment as a twenty-two-year-old subaltern. A good linguist, a sportsman (and at 6 foot 4 a talented goalkeeper), he did well as a junior officer. His quirky sense of humour made him popular with his peers, while his love of classical music, his restless intelligence and a wide reading that ran to serial enthusiasm for the philosophers Nietzsche, Bergson and Schopenhauer marked him out from his peers. He was not conventionally ambitious, often telling colleagues he would sooner be a postman in Norfolk than a general in India.

Hugh Seagrim turned out to be a natural regimental soldier, a gifted trainer and leader of men. He got to know the Karens, and they him; and for the rest of his life he was to serve with them. His quick mastery of languages – he spoke fluent Burmese and some Karen too – impressed them, as did his goal-keeping and his height. In his last letter to his mother he wrote that there was a chance he 'wouldn't get through', and that if he did not he 'wanted to leave a memory with the Karens'.

The Karens in Burma were an ethnic and religious minority who had long been subjugated and distrusted by the dominant Buddhist Burmese. Some Karens, particularly their leaders, had embraced Christianity as a result of US missionary work from 1813. Indeed it was said that the Karens called the American missionaries their 'mother', and the British authorities their 'father'. In the nineteenth century they had welcomed the arrival of the British, whom they saw as advancing their rights in Burma.

Most Karens lived a village life, agrarian and simple, and were led by tribal elders. Those from the mountains of Salween province in the east of Burma, the 'hill Karens', were strongly represented in the Burma Rifles, among whom they were valued as tough and trustworthy soldiers. It was from this regiment that Seagrim was eventually to raise his irregular force, the Karen Levies. In the late 1930s, when Japan and China were fighting to the east of Burma, he recognised the Karens' potential for guerrilla warfare against any enemy, and considered the Indian Army's traditional drill-based approach to training to be pointless, even irrelevant, for the threats ahead.

Japan's attack on British, American and Dutch possessions in the Far East in 1941 was followed by a series of rapid Japanese advances across South-East Asia. In Burma preparations were made for resistance against an enemy that possessed overwhelming advantages, in both numbers and air superiority; plans for Operation Oriental Mission, which would impose maximum delay upon the Japanese 'by using forces other than regular forces', also began to be laid.

The leader of Operation Oriental Mission quickly saw the need to employ Seagrim – who had long argued for the raising, training and use of an army of Karen irregulars – and he was seconded to the new force. Seagrim was delighted to join it. Gradually its role was defined: in 'stay-behind' units, it would attack Japanese supply routes such as the Moulmein–Rangoon road and railway.

What was sound in theory proved almost impossible in practice. The main problem was a desperate shortage of arms and ammunition, and time was running out. The Japanese were advancing from Siam into Burma. In late January 1942 Seagrim set out for Papun, in the mountains of Salween province, with a collection of miscellaneous firearms, a few tommy guns and some grenades. A small supply convoy, bringing a couple hundred Italian rifles and a few thousand rounds of ammunition, arrived a few days later; on its return to Rangoon it was almost cut off by the rapidly advancing enemy.

In Papun, Seagrim recruited 200 levies and trained them in the way he had always advocated, despite the doctrine. Barefoot, and encouraged to shoot accurately from any position which they found comfortable, they practised concealment and ambush techniques in the hill country they knew well. Seagrim's army colleague, Ronald Heath, later a successful jungle training officer with the Chindits, was impressed by the results. He said of Seagrim: 'Any of those Karen boys would have done anything for him. He had a terrific sway over those lads.'

With the Japanese having overrun Burma, Seagrim and his contingent of Karens proved to be active and disruptive behind enemy lines. Seagrim was now, however, in continuous danger. He moved north for safety; the last British official he spoke to before he set off found him 'cheerful, but not betting on his chances'. In the northern hills he took to wearing Karen attire. There he trained and organised several hundred more recruits, but the shortage of weapons and ammunition with which to train was a grave drawback. In desperation, the Karen crossbow, fatal at up to 75 yards, became a weapon of modern war.

As restricting as the lack of stores and firepower was the lack of communication with the outside world. In April, Seagrim, who had once served as a signals officer, set out to obtain a wireless set from forces in a town to the north, but discovered when he got there that the Japanese were in control. On the way back he was wounded in an ambush by local non-Karen tribesmen, and spent the next four months hidden in the jungle recuperating in the care of two Karen pastors, and using the time to brush up on his theology.

Recovered, though still lacking arms, ammunition and communications, Seagrim continued to sustain the morale and loyalty of his levies across a vast territory, maintaining contact through messengers, and endlessly at risk of betrayal through any breach of security. Sustained and concealed by the Karens – who said of him: 'He has learned to live like us' – Seagrim moved from village to village, hut to hut, seeking out veterans of the Burma Rifles, registering their names, and making plans to support British troops once they returned to Burma. Operation Oriental Mission had become little more than a holding operation, but Seagrim never gave up.

In late 1942 British and Indian forces were once more on the offensive in the Arakan, and GHQ in Delhi looked again at the possibility of irregular operations behind Japanese lines in the Karen hill country. Early in

1943, three officers, two British and one Karen, volunteered to be parachuted in, with communication equipment and instructions to make contact with Seagrim, who was assumed – somewhat against the odds – to be still alive. There were many attempts, but eventual success: in October 1943 Major Nimmo and Lieutenant Ba Gyaw linked up with Seagrim and established wireless communication with India. At last useful intelligence traffic began to flow into Delhi.

Word of parachute drops and the presence of British officers in the Karen hills reached the Japanese, and early in 1944 a seventeen-man Japanese 'Goods Distribution Unit' arrived in Papun and sold matches and cloth at suspiciously low rates. They were in fact a military unit looking for Seagrim. Casual enquiries about foreign soldiers and parachute drops confirmed suspicions, which loyal Karens passed to Seagrim, who moved camp further into the mountains. Shortly afterwards, the Japanese, who had learned of the activities of Po Hla, a Karen friend and supporter of Seagrim who had family in Rangoon, informed him through a distant relative that if he did not hand himself in his family would suffer. The net was closing in.

Soon Japanese infantry and military police units appeared in force in the Karen hills and began arresting and torturing suspects, including Maung Wah, an old Burma Rifles veteran who was one of Seagrim's levy commanders. Maung Wah endured three days of beating and revealed nothing. When he was eventually released, he went into the hills to tell Seagrim, who was once more on his own, what was happening. Seagrim wept, but the old soldier simply entreated him to signal for aid and arms from India and start a Karen revolt. Seagrim tried, but GHQ in Delhi refused, arguing that the time was not ripe.

Others under torture told more, and soon the Japanese knew all they needed: about the levies, the arms dumps and about Seagrim's whereabouts. Although loyal Karens still kept Seagrim informed, and although he continued to move camp, nothing could be done to prevent the Japanese locating him and launching an attack. Seagrim and most of his companions were alerted by the noisy Japanese approach, and escaped. In the following search of the mountainous jungle site, Captain Inoue, leader of a unit of the much-feared *Kempeitai* (military police), found Seagrim's Bible. Seagrim himself remained at large for another month.

The Japanese were determined to find Seagrim; their actions in the Karen hills degenerated into a reign of terror. The loyalty and silence of the Karens resulted in Japanese reprisals that were savage and brutally systematic. Karen villages were burned and elders were tortured, sometimes to death. Innocent people suffered dreadfully for what was, in the eyes of their oppressors, treachery: they had hidden and protected an Allied agent.

Meanwhile, Seagrim and Pa Ah, a young Karen who had been parachuted in from India, made their way through twenty-five miles of jungle to Mewado, a village where Pa Ah's brother-in-law fed and protected them. They stayed in the hills, with food brought to them every few days; but the Japanese again closed in, looking for Pa Ah, whom they knew had family in the area. Under threat, the villagers persuaded him to give himself up. While Pa Ah was in Japanese custody, word of Seagrim's whereabouts reached Captain Inoue.

When Inoue arrived with the *Kempeitai* at Mewado he threatened to burn down the village and arrest its inhabitants. The headman, by now a friend of Seagrim, offered to go and talk to him the next day. They discussed suicide, which Seagrim rejected as un-Christian. He decided instead to give himself up, to end the suffering being inflicted on the Karen by the Japanese. As they walked to the village Seagrim gave the head man his watch, asking him to send it to his mother in England after the war.

In Mewado, Seagrim and Inoue shook hands. Seagrim smoked his first cigarette for two years but declined the offer of a whole packet. He then asked Inoue to treat the Karens generously, telling him: 'They are not to blame. I alone am responsible for what has happened in the hills.' Captor and captive then spent several days together, sharing meals and accommodation and talking at length through an interpreter, with Seagrim repeating his pleas for clemency towards the Karens. Inoue returned Seagrim's Bible, and heard of his plans to be a missionary among the Karens if he survived the war.

On 16 March 1944 Seagrim was taken from Papun, first in an oxcart, then by train, to Rangoon, where he was held prisoner at the *Kempeitai* headquarters – a grim jail where torture was common and many died. Seagrim stood out there, not simply because of his height: a fellow prisoner, Arthur Sharpe, a young RAF officer shot down over Burma, found in him 'a profound philosophy and a strong religious faith'. He was, he said, 'the finest gentleman I have ever met. He had a complete disregard for his own life and at the same time the greatest concern for the Karen NCOs and men under him.'

While in jail Seagrim conducted a short service for an RAF officer who had died. The service included an impromptu prayer. 'Nothing could reveal better this man's wonderful character than those words which are now lost,' wrote Sharpe. 'A tribute to the dead, a prayer for the living, and, greatest of all, a word for his cruel captors . . . he said, in the words of Christ: "Lord, forgive them, for they know not what they do".'

In early July, Seagrim and the surviving hill Karens in captivity were transferred to another jail at Insein near Rangoon. On 2 September he and fifteen Karens were summoned to a court martial. Again Seagrim pleaded for the lives of the Karens, saying that he alone was responsible for their actions, and that he alone should suffer. He and seven of the Karens were sentenced to death; the remaining eight received long jail sentences.

As the condemned men were driven away, with Seagrim still wearing the Karen attire he had worn since March 1942, one Karen witness noted that, as he shouted goodbye to those destined only to jail, he was 'smiley-faced'. The citation for his posthumous George Cross reads: 'There can hardly be a finer example of self-sacrifice and bravery than that exhibited by this officer who in cold blood deliberately gave himself up to save others, knowing well what his fate was likely to be at the hands of the enemy.'

The Japanese had prevailed over Seagrim and his Karen levies. But within a year of his death it was clear that his courage, leadership and ultimate sacrifice with and for the Karens had made possible a sustained, massive military offensive that owed much to him and his work in the hills. Operation Character, which began in April 1945, was the largest and most successful example of irregular warfare in all South-East Asia Command. As Slim's epic Fourteenth Army offensive of early 1945 unfolded, more than 12,000 Karens, by then well armed and properly supported, wrought havoc on the Japanese forces in Burma until the Japanese surrender in Burma in May. Seagrim's faith in the Karens had been more than vindicated. In the words he used in his last letter to his mother, he had truly succeeded in leaving 'a memory with the Karens'.

9

Fame, Faith and Courage

Eric Liddell

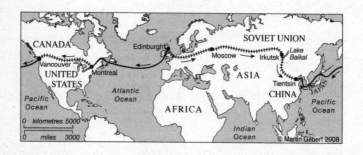

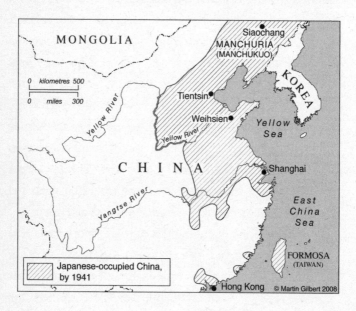

E ric Liddell is best remembered today as the Scottish student who won a gold medal with a record-breaking time in the 400 metres at the 1924 Paris Olympics; and as the man of principle who refused to run on a Sunday even when that meant missing his strongest event, the 100 metres sprint. The story was immortalised in the 1981 film *Chariots of Fire* and his fame spread around the world. Far less well known is his subsequent life: as a teacher and missionary and then as an inspirational leader in a Japanese internment camp in China, where he died at the age of forty-three, just six months before he would have been liberated with his fellow internees as the Second World War ended.

His phenomenal public success as a sportsman and athlete – he played international rugby as well as winning Olympic gold – lasted only a few years, from 1921 to 1924. Immediately afterwards he trained for missionary work, then served for ten years in China as a teacher at the Anglo-Chinese College of the London Missionary Society at Tientsin, before undertaking much more demanding and dangerous work in northern China during the Sino-Japanese war. When, following Japanese attacks on Hong Kong and Pearl Harbor in December 1941, Japan and Britain were at war, Liddell was subjected to increasing restrictions as an enemy alien in Japanese-occupied China, and ultimately to great deprivation and hardship in captivity with 1,500 other civilians under the Japanese in a camp at Weihsien until his death in February 1945. His achievement as an athlete won him public acclaim, and he inspired millions; what we witness in his wartime courage is quite different and even more inspiring: quiet sustained altruism and leadership of the highest order.

However distinguished his sporting career and his triumph in Paris, Liddell always regarded his missionary work as 'the greater race'. The same faith, self-sacrifice and determination that took him to the top in world athletics was tested again and again in the remaining twenty years of his life. It was never found wanting. His courage in some of the most difficult circumstances encountered by non-combatants in the Second World War was unfailing, and deserves to be far better known.

Eric Henry Liddell was of missionary stock. He was born in China and had his early upbringing there. His parents were Scottish. His father, James, was from Stirlingshire and trained at the Scottish Congregational

College; ordained in 1898, he joined the London Missionary Society, a non-denominational evangelical group that had been active in China since the mid-nineteenth century. His mother, Mary, from the Scottish Borders, had trained as a nurse. She and James married in Shanghai in 1899. Eric, their second son, was born on 16 January 1902 in Tientsin, a busy Chinese river town with a large population and established European trading settlements. Subsequently the family moved north to a remote mission station at Siaochang, where Eric himself was to serve many years later.

The scale, ethos and culture of the overseas missionary work based in Britain in the nineteenth and early twentieth century is now largely forgotten. Great demands were made of those who took part in it. Transport was slow and communications were poor. Decades of service abroad were broken by occasional prolonged periods of leave, called furlough, which were taken in the home country. Family separation was routine and accepted. Children were sent home for education, and suitable schools and even university accommodation were dedicated for the use of the offspring of missionary families.

Eric Liddell attended one such school, Eltham College in Kent, and did well there. Sport and intellectual activity were both encouraged. Eric was bright as well as athletic, gaining university entrance qualifications and being spotted as a talented runner. His older brother Rob had gone from Eltham to Edinburgh University to read medicine with a view to missionary work, and Eric followed him there to read chemistry. On a townhouse at 56 George Square, once the Edinburgh Medical Missionary Hostel but now just another set of university offices, there is a plaque which reads: 'In honour of Eric H. Liddell 1902–1945 Olympic 400 metres champion (1924), graduate of the University, teacher and missionary, who lived here from 1922 to 1924.'

Though he was to find fame as an athlete and serve with great distinction as a missionary, his approach to both was tentative. He required some persuasion to participate in athletics at Edinburgh, and lagged behind his older brother in religious zeal until quite late in his university career. But the talented schoolboy runner quickly came to dominate student track events. At the university sports in May 1921, Liddell, a newcomer, beat the 1920 sprint champion in both the 100 and 220 yards. Later that year, he swept all before him at the Scottish Inter-University Sports in Glasgow; and in all his appearances in university-level track events he came first in all but one race he entered.

With a record like that, the 'flying Scotsman', as Liddell quickly became known, soon took on international competition. At the English Amateur Athletic Association meeting at Stamford Bridge in 1923 runners from Britain and abroad competed. In the 100 and 220 yards Liddell came first in every heat he entered, as well as in both finals. It was there that he first met Harold Abrahams, the rival who was also to find fame in *Chariots of Fire*. Soon afterwards, at an international track event held at Stoke-on-Trent, Liddell sustained a minor injury during the 440 yards when he was jostled on the track; he stumbled, re-entered the race some distance behind, and still won a narrow victory over the Englishman who had nearly pushed him out of contention – an outcome all the more remarkable for Liddell having achieved it in borrowed running shoes. A version of that incident and Liddell's heroic recovery from it appears in the film.

Less well known, though no less astonishing, is Liddell's brief career as a rugby player. He had done his bit for his school at Eltham as captain of the 1st XV, but went on to excel at Edinburgh. At 5 foot 9 and weighing 155lbs, and with unmatched speed, he appeared as a wing three-quarter for Scotland in the 1921–22 season after only three months in the senior game. The following season with the Scottish team Liddell scored tries in successive victories against France, Wales and Ireland. In the last international – against England at Inverleith in March 1923 – Scotland missed the Grand Slam title by only two points, going down 6–8 to 'the old enemy', with Liddell yet again scoring a try. In the little world of

Edinburgh University, where there were then only a few thousand students, he had become not just a major celebrity but also – to use another term not then invented – a sporting superstar.

The culmination of his athletics career – his appearance and victory in the 400 metres at the Paris Olympics of 1924 – is well documented, as is the strict Sabbatarianism which kept him out the 100 metres and the 4 x 400 metres relay, both of which involved racing on a Sunday. Liddell's evangelical missionary background made his observance of Sunday as a day of rest inevitable; it was, and remained, a lifetime commitment, determined from the start by family and faith. It went with his other strict personal habits: he never smoked and never touched alcohol, once describing himself as a 'third or fourth generation teetotaller and non-smoker'.

Liddell had known for months that the shorter distances in the Paris Olympics were not for him, and so he trained hard for the 400 metres. His previously excellent academic record – he had regularly come top or near it in the exams for his various university courses – suffered as a result. But coached by a professional, and committed to his training, he was thoroughly prepared for his Olympic appearance, entering both the 200 (in which he eventually took the bronze) and the 400 metres.

Though a little-known competitor over that distance at international level, Liddell showed his potential in the second semi-final of the 400 metres, winning it in a personal best and near record-breaking time of 48.1 seconds. When the finalists lined up, at least one of them might have appreciated the band and music accompanying them on the field: the pipes and drums of the Queen's Own Cameron Highlanders playing 'Scotland the Brave'. The 'flying Scotsman' duly lived up to his reputation, swiftly covering the first 200 metres and still increasing his lead over the last fifty. His time, 47.6 seconds, was a world and Olympic record. It was a perfect race and the gold medal was his, but Eric Liddell was already set on higher things.

As the son of missionaries, brought up in a missionary compound in China and schooled at Eltham, he had from the first the faith and outlook of an evangelical Christian, and the expectation too that he would one day become a missionary also. Not long after winning the 400 metres in Paris he spoke about that vocation:

It's been a wonderful experience to compete in the Olympic games and to bring home a gold medal. But since I have been a young lad I have had my eyes on a different prize. You see, each of us is in a greater race than any I have run in Paris . . . It was always my intention to be a missionary, and I have just received word that I have been accepted as a chemistry teacher at the Anglo-Chinese College in Tientsin, China. From now on I will be putting my energy into preparing to take up that position.

When he graduated from Edinburgh with a BSc in chemistry only weeks after his Olympic triumph, Liddell was singled out by the university for unique treatment. This included a wreath of olive leaves and a congratulatory scroll, and even a bad joke from the principal ('It was clear that no one could pass Liddell but his examiners . . .'). Afterwards he was carried shoulder-high by fellow students to a church service in St Giles's cathedral, but none of that went to his head or tempted him from his chosen path. He spent the following year as a student at the Congregational College in Edinburgh preparing for his work as a missionary. His studies were supplemented by field-work: speaking at missions and addressing meetings in various Scottish towns.

One series of Edinburgh meetings culminated in a Sunday evening gathering in the Usher Hall, which he was to address. Such was his reputation that it was hugely oversubscribed, mainly by students, and an over-flow meeting had to be arranged in a nearby church. And, as with his graduation, Eric Liddell's departure for China on completion of his training in the summer of

1925 became a public event. Farewell meetings were held, and fellow students pulled him in a decorated open carriage more than two miles from the Congregational College to Waverley train station. A young man of outstanding athletic and sporting prowess, already endowed with a charisma that would mark him out wherever he went, had set himself upon a course that would lead to privation, sacrifice, separation from loved ones, danger, and death in a prison camp on the other side of the world.

After saying goodbye to his mother's family in the Borders, he went south to London, by ferry to Holland, then by train to Moscow, and by the Trans-Siberian railway to China, where he was reunited with his parents at Tientsin in mid-July. After a period of familiarisation and time spent beginning to re-learn the second language of his boyhood, he took up his post at the Anglo-Chinese College of the London Missionary Society, a boys' school with some 500 pupils drawn from the Chinese and European communities of Tientsin. He taught chemistry, and – inevitably, given his record – coached pupils in both athletics and team sports. He took Bible study, and became Sunday school superintendent in the church where his father, who had retired in 1929, had been the minister, and was himself ordained. He was to stay at Tientsin for ten years.

Not long after his arrival in Tientsin, Liddell met a Canadian girl, the daughter of a missionary family, who was ten years his junior. The relationship endured her departure to her homeland to train as a nurse, and was rekindled on her return. Eric Henry Liddell was married to Florence MacKenzie in Tientsin in 1934. Theirs was a happy union, with a shared faith and a strong commitment to the missionary life. A family soon followed, with two daughters born within a few years and another later, in 1941, who would never see her father.

By 1937 their life together, and indeed the whole missionary enterprise, was under serious threat. An international conflict between China and Japan that had been simmering since the Japanese had set up a puppet regime in Manchuria in 1932 broke out into open warfare in 1937. From that year until 1945 much of northern China was fought over as Japanese invading forces met opposition from both Communist and Nationalist Chinese armies who were already fighting each other. Law and order broke down and brigandage was widespread. In the countryside north of Tientsin mission stations and their surrounding communities of Christian Chinese were under great pressure; missionaries willing to serve there were few and far between. The London Missionary Society approached Eric, raising the possibility that he might leave the city and minister to those out in the war-torn countryside.

After much thought and some hesitation, Eric Liddell, with the prayerful support of his wife, decided to go north and return to Siaochang, the missionary outpost where he had spent his early childhood. Siaochang had become a war zone, which meant leaving Florence and the two girls in Tientsin. It was a difficult decision and he agonised over it. He felt 'more equipped for educational work both by training and temperament', and had grave doubts about his abilities as a rural missionary; but he felt also the call of duty, though the presence of his older brother Rob, by then a medical missionary and the hospital superintendent at Siaochang, might also have been a factor.

The Siaochang mission supported evangelical work in thousands of villages across a territory encompassing several thousand square miles. Eric based himself in the mission compound that had been his home thirty years earlier, and even inherited the Chinese name, Li Mu Shi – a rough phonetic approximation of the first syllable of their surname and the first two syllables of 'missionary' – once bestowed on his father. Conditions were just as bad as expected: transport was primitive and the roads were dire, so that Eric and his interpreter did most of their travelling by bicycle. Determined, and still very fit, he again thrived on challenge, tackling his huge commitments with skill and zeal; going from village to village, from church to church, holding regular conferences with Chinese preachers, and preaching and winning new converts himself. In a letter to a mutual friend, Florence wrote: 'He felt God was calling him to the country, and I think it was obvious he did the right thing. He loved the work, his health improved, and I think he blossomed out in a new way.'

In 1939 he took his second and, as it turned out, his last furlough, undertaking various mission-related duties in Britain, meeting Florence and the two girls in Scotland, and then, in March 1940, heading west with them across the Atlantic to Canada, in a convoy which came under submarine attack resulting in the loss of several ships. By the end of the year they were back in Tientsin, but in 1941 learned that the mission station at Siaochang was no more: it had been devastated by enemy action. Shortly afterwards Florence and the girls left for Canada. They would never see Eric again.

With the coming of war between Japan and Britain in December 1941, and with Japanese forces occupying Tientsin, the British missionaries there had become enemy aliens and were treated accordingly. No further meaningful missionary work was possible; meetings of more than ten people were banned, and foreigners were subject to increasingly harsh restrictions. Any hopes Liddell had of leaving China and rejoining his family in Canada faded during 1942, and in March 1943 all enemy nationals in Tientsin were told to prepare for internment in a camp at Weihsien 400 miles away. Instructions were issued about permitted luggage, and three parties would travel on successive days by rail.

The precise arrangements were clearly intended to assert both the dominance of the Japanese and the humiliation of their Westerner captives, who had to report with their belongings at the Tientsin recreation grounds and then, following an inspection by their captors, walk under guard from there to the French Concession, on towards the Bund and then across the International Bridge to the railway station. Crowds watched them in silence, and Japanese photographers were on hand to take propaganda pictures: the old order had changed, and the Tokyo newspapers would have proof of it.

On 31 March 1943, after a long and extremely uncomfortable overnight journey in an overcrowded train, Liddell, designated 'captain' of the third and last contingent, arrived at Weihsien internment camp. It was a former American Presbyterian missionary base with a large sign at the gate that read: 'Courtyard of the Happy Way'. Within a perimeter fence topped with barbed wire and watched by armed sentries, accommodation blocks, housing 1,500 inmates, were arranged along little streets with names as incongruous as the sign at the gate: Sunset Boulevard, Acacia Court, Park Avenue, and the like.

The new internees from Tientsin were first lined up in the camp church, where the Japanese commandant read out the regulations and warned that any non-compliance would be severely dealt with. As they settled in they got to know their fellow prisoners, many of whom had been there for months. Though they spoke with familiar accents – British, American, European – they were emaciated, deeply tanned and barefoot; it took the newcomers very little time to realise that soon they too would look like that.

Rations were meagre and sporadic, and cooking arrangements entirely a matter for the prisoners. There were roll-calls twice a day, strictly carried out and often prolonged, but otherwise the internees were left largely to their own devices within the camp. Gradually they organised themselves, making use of their skills and previous experience to provide a makeshift school for the children, a hospital of sorts, and a variety of recreational and religious activities.

Again Liddell was given a position of responsibility, as roll-call warden for Blocks 23 and 24; but it is clear from the memoirs of those who survived that, while his health held out, he did far more than account twice daily to the Japanese for those in his charge. He was ceaselessly active in the care and support of his fellow prisoners, attending to practical as well as to spiritual needs, and tireless in inspiring and organising others to do likewise.

One survivor described how 'Liddell seemed to be ubiquitous – he was all over the camp, holding friendly conversations with all kinds of people . . .' He drew on his past to help younger internees cope with the frustrations of confinement: 'Soon he was organising races . . . He also organised hockey matches, and was known to have repaired the hockey sticks by tearing up his own bed sheets.' Though there was almost no equipment Liddell gave science classes in the school, using a textbook he had written from memory; despite everything his students learned well, with some going on with science after the war ended. He carried water for the sick and elderly; and once set up a bookshelf for a Russian prostitute, who later said he was the only person in her entire life who had done something nice for her without asking anything in return. 'In the end, people from all walks of life loved Eric for his genuine, unselfish love,' another former internee recalled.

Every Sunday afternoon about a hundred children came to his Sunday school, and there were weeknight meetings in the church at which Liddell often spoke. His preaching was remembered as 'simple, direct and supported by homely illustrations', and was all the more effective because what he said was reflected in everything he did: he 'lived out the Sermon on the Mount'. He served also as a counsellor, with one survivor recalling how 'when personal relationships got just too impossible, he had a gentle, humorous way of soothing ruffled tempers and bringing to one's mind some by-gone happiness, or the prospect of some future interest round the corner "when we get out".'

Eric Liddell never got out of the Weihsien camp. Early in 1945 his characteristic energy began to fail and friends noticed a change in his personality. He complained of headaches, then showed signs of a possible stroke. A brain tumour was diagnosed. Soon he was confined to the camp infirmary and declined quickly thereafter. He died on 21 February 1945.

Shortly before he died, he requested a hymn. Some of Liddell's friends, who had formed a Salvation Army band, were playing outside the infirmary when a nurse passed a note out of the window: 'Eric would like you to play "Finlandia".' As they obliged, they were thinking, as Liddell almost certainly was too, of the words usually sung to that tune:

> Be still, my soul. The Lord is thy side;
> Bear patiently the cross of grief or pain.
> Leave to thy God to order and provide;
> In every change He faithful will remain.
> Be still, my soul, thy best, thy heavenly Friend
> Through thorny ways leads to a joyful end.

Virtually the whole camp turned out for Liddell's funeral service and followed his coffin up the hill to the cemetery. A whole community had lost a friend, pastor, and leader. Eric Liddell's direct contributions to the welfare of hundreds of internees had been untiring and utterly selfless, providing care, support and comfort. His influence for good – through his leadership and, above all, through his example – had been incalculable. Every traceable memoir by anyone who survived internment in Weihsien records some kindness, inspiring word, or achievement for the common good on the part of the former Olympic athlete who had worked and died among them.

His grave was marked with a wooden cross that bore his name written in black shoe polish. No trace of that cross, or indeed of the cemetery, remains today, but a memorial stone in red granite, brought from the Isle of Mull, was unveiled in 1991 on the site of the camp and in the presence of a number of Weihsien survivors. It bears a fitting text, from Isaiah, chapter 40, verse 31: 'They shall mount up with wings as eagles; they shall run and not be weary.'

10

The Home Front

*Harry Errington, Ben Gimbert
and Jim Nightall*

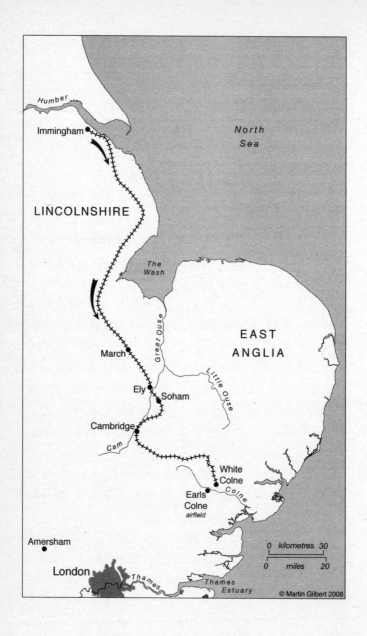

Humber

Immingham

North
Sea

LINCOLNSHIRE

The
Wash

Great Ouse

March

EAST
ANGLIA

Little Ouse

Ely Soham

Cambridge

Cam

White
Colne

Colne

Earls
Colne
airfield

Amersham

London

Thames

Thames
Estuary

0   kilometres 30
0   miles   20

© Martin Gilbert 2008

The London Blitz – Germany's bombing offensive against Britain's capital city – began on 7 September 1940. In the wake of the Luftwaffe's defeat in the Battle of Britain that autumn, and with the Royal Navy still in command of the sea, Germany was compelled to seek other means of attack against its sole remaining adversary. For almost every day of the subsequent two months, German bombers appeared over London in a sustained attempt to disrupt the life of the capital, to destroy its administrative centre and its vital docks, and to demoralise and subdue its people. By the end of May 1941, when the squadrons of Heinkels and Dornier bombers and their escorting fighters were moved east to support the invasion of Russia, a million houses in London had been destroyed or damaged, and 20,000 Londoners had been killed.

Such attacks had long been anticipated, and preparations made to deal with them. Not all these preparations proved effective. Anti-aircraft guns in the early stages were too few and lacked range, as did the searchlights that were meant to identify their targets. And, although daylight raids could be countered by RAF Fighter Command, there was as yet little in the way of night-fighting capability. For two months regular day and night raids, by bombers numbering anything from 100 to 400, took a regular toll in destruction, injury, and death.

Pre-war predictions of the effects of bombing on large cities eventually proved over-pessimistic, but they had had a salutary influence on advance planning for civil defence. From the time of the Munich crisis in September 1938 and on through the long months of the 'phoney war' from September the following year, a broadly effective system of air-raid precautions and air-raid shelters had been developed in the capital. Fire had been anticipated as the major risk – the majority of the bombs dropped were indeed incendiaries – and so the normal peacetime manpower and resources of the London Fire Brigade had been greatly augmented by a new voluntary wartime organisation, the Auxiliary Fire Service, the AFS, founded at the end of 1938.

AFS firemen were civilian volunteers who undertook training for fire-fighting and rescue work. All their training sessions, and their responses to emergencies once the bombing had begun, were commitments additional to their normal civilian employment. Lawyers, office workers, tradesmen, shopkeepers and artisans joined in their thousands. Many who were too old or too young for military service took part, as did many in reserved occupations who were ineligible for call-up. Equipment was in short supply, and often improvised; many of the AFS 'fire engines' were in fact ordinary London taxi cabs, painted grey instead of black to denote their new emergency role.

AFS fire-fighting teams and the accompanying AFS light and heavy rescue units became a vital and effective force in the defence of Britain's capital, but the AFS paid the price in casualties. Several thousand firefighters were seriously injured, and more than 300 lost their lives.

On the night of 17 September 1940, a detachment of AFS firefighters was on duty in a makeshift air-raid shelter in the basement of a three-storey commercial building, then the Rathbone Street AFS Sub-Fire Station in Soho, just north of Oxford Street in the West End of London. Shortly before midnight, a direct hit by a high-explosive bomb caused the building to collapse and set the ruins on fire: twenty people, seven of them firemen, were killed.

In the basement of the shattered building, Harry Errington, a thirty-year-old firefighter and master cutter for a Savile Row tailor, was knocked out by the blast. When he recovered consciousness, he found a fierce fire spreading. As he headed for the emergency exit he heard the desperate cries of two members of his watch, trapped under the debris.

Errington turned back, found a blanket, soaked it in water, and covered his head and shoulders. Then, with the small protection that it offered from the smoke, heat and flames, he set about trying to extricate the trapped men. Using only a fire axe and his bare hands – which were burned in the process – he managed to pull the first of them free. This man was unable to walk, so Errington hauled him up the basement stairs, into a courtyard and on to the relative safety of the street. He then returned for the second man, who was trapped under a heavy radiator, freed him, and carried him up to safety.

All three men had suffered burns, but all three returned to their AFS duties within a few weeks. One of those saved was a solicitor, John Terry, who was later knighted for his services as managing director of the National Film Finance Corporation from 1958 to 1978. The three, together with their families, remained firm friends, keeping in touch over the decades.

For Harry Errington's selfless courage that night, he was awarded the George Cross. It was announced in the *London Gazette* in August 1941. In October 1942, he attended an investiture and received his medal from King George VI. He was the only London fireman to receive the George Cross, and one of only three firemen thus honoured.

Harry Errington was born in Soho on 20 August 1910 to a Jewish family from Poland who had anglicised their name from Ehregott. After attending the Westminster free school, he joined his uncle's small tailoring business. He would remain with the firm throughout his working life, retiring in 1992 as a director of Errington and Whyte, by then in Savile Row.

Errington's other main interest was basketball, in which he was a successful coach and then manager: in later life he was vice-chairman, and then life vice-president, of the UK Amateur Basketball Association. He also served as a committee member of the VC and GC Association for more than thirty years, and was its honorary treasurer for twelve.

In 1995 he attended the service at St Paul's Cathedral commemorating the defeat of Germany fifty years earlier. When asked by a bystander, who recognised his George Cross medal, what he had done he said he had only acted as any fireman would have done.

He kept in touch with fire-fighting, often calling in at his local fire station in Soho. In August 2000, that fire station's Red Watch threw a party for him to celebrate his ninetieth birthday. He died, aged ninety-four, on 15 December 2004.

Shortly afterwards, in January 2005, Dr Julian Lewis, MP, tabled an early day motion in the House of Commons. It read:

That this House salutes the passing of Harry Errington, the British-born son of Polish immigrants, who won the George Cross at the height of the London Blitz when, as a volunteer firefighter, he saved the lives of two trapped comrades in circumstances of great danger; recalls the sacrifice of over 300 firefighters who lost their lives in the London region alone; and pays tribute to all who manned the emergency services throughout countless attacks upon the United Kingdom during the Second World War.

A little less than four years after the end of the London Blitz, the overall war situation had been transformed. Though in early June 1944 the German aerial attack on London continued – then in the form of V1 flying bombs and V2 rockets – the Allied bomber offensive on occupied Europe had assumed huge proportions. From 150 airfields, mainly in the southeast of England, RAF Bomber Command and US 8th Air Force bomber squadrons continued to pound German war production and – without giving away too much about the location of the impending D-Day landings in Normandy – were carrying out daily operations designed to cripple the German response to the landings, with a focus on the transport network, and in particular the railways of northern France.

Britain's railways also played a major part in the Second World War: a contribution that is often overlooked. They provided the principal means of transporting troops and war materials on a scale far exceeding that achieved in the First World War; and – with the bomber offensive approaching its greatest intensity, and this coinciding with the vast troop and munitions movements in the run-up to D-Day – by 1944 the railways' contribution to the war was reaching its peak.

Britain's railway system had worked well throughout the war. Damage to it from air raids was expected and had been planned for; when it occurred the civil engineering department reacted swiftly and effectively, often beginning repairs to tracks, stations and marshalling yards even before the all clear was sounded. More than a million goods wagons were controlled as a single resource from an office in Amersham, Buckinghamshire, with such efficiency that by 1943 military freight had risen by 50 per cent with no increase in the number of wagons in use. This was a remarkable achievement, which was sustained into 1944 despite the increasing use of single-track rural lines to minor south coast ports, and to the bomber airfields scattered throughout East Anglia and Lincolnshire.

On 31 May 1944 a consignment of bombs from the United States was unloaded from a munitions ship docked at Immingham on the Humber estuary, and transferred to a sixty-one-wagon train. Hauled by a newly built 128-ton coal-fired '2-8-0' steam engine, its main destination was White Colne station, near Earls Colne airfield, Colchester, Essex – home of the USAAF's 323rd Bombardment Group (Medium), whose B-26 Marauders were already engaging D-Day-related targets in northern France and Belgium.

The train, with thousands of bombs on board, set out from Immingham in the early hours of 1 June. Its first stop was the marshalling yard at March, Cambridgeshire, 90 miles away, where it arrived after seven hours – a time that reflected the great care with which such dangerous loads were handled. Explosives, in the main body of the bombs, travelled in wagons separately from the fins, primers and detonators; low-combustibility tarpaulin covered each load – an important precaution in the era of coal-fired steam engines – and all ammunition trains were checked regularly and in detail at every stop.

During the fourteen-hour stop at March the train was reduced for the next stage of its journey to fifty-one wagons. By then only 390 metres long, it consisted of forty-four wagons laden with unarmed 250-pound and 500-pound bombs and the remaining wagons carrying the separately handled components. At 12.15 a.m. on 2 June it left March as the delayed 11.40 p.m. (1 June) to White Colne. It was checked shortly afterwards at a stop in Ely, with nothing found amiss. Signals were clear for the journey down a single-track line to the small country town of Soham, where the line became double again. On the single-track line the train proceeded cautiously at between 15 and 20 miles an hour.

The engine driver, Ben Gimbert, aged forty-one, was experienced. Alongside him on the footplate was Jim Nightall, his fireman, who was much younger. In the guard's van nearly a quarter of a mile behind the engine was the train guard, Herbert Clarke – at fifty-nine the veteran of the crew. In the signal-box at Soham station, just short of the station itself, was Frank 'Sailor' Bridges, known to Gimbert from his regular duties on the Soham line.

Ben Gimbert's report of what followed appeared soon afterwards in a local newspaper:

Before anything else I must speak about my mate Jim Nightall, who was killed. He was only twenty-two and he died doing his duty as coolly as any older, more experienced man. And 'Sailor' Bridges, the dead signalman, he was the same. Jim and I were on the footplate as we approached the station where the explosion happened. Looking back along the train . . . I saw flames coming from the bottom of the first bomb truck. I've never thought so quickly or clearly before.

I knew that if I stopped the train with a jerk, all the trucks of ammunition might explode. It had to be a smooth pull-up without any banging about. I told myself I had to keep calm, and I brought the train to a standstill. As we stopped I shouted to my mate 'uncouple the wagons, Jim, take the coal hammer with you in case the coupling is hot'. Nightall didn't turn a hair and didn't hesitate or ask any questions. He jumped straight down on the track and I ran round to help him. Bridges was out of his signal box running to help us.

In a minute the train was uncoupled. I started the engine again pulling the burning wagon behind me. Jim was by my side. The flames were quite high around the wagon then, and I knew that we had to hurry. Everything was so peaceful and still. The town was in darkness, and I thought of all the sleeping women and kids, and the 50 trucks of bombs behind us. I thought that I must stick to the engine until I could get clear of the town, and I was just opening the throttle when I remembered that the mail express train was almost due on that line.

What I did next may have saved my life. I went to the right of my cab and shouted to the signalman, 'Frank – stop the mail! Stop the mail, while I get clear!' He began running to his box to make sure the mail would not come by, and I remember turning back to the engine, looking at the fire and starting to pull-off away from the station. I knew those bombs were due to explode. That was all I remember. Next, I was staggering about on a roadway some distance from the track, and I felt a lot of pain. A soldier came up to me. I asked him about my mate and then I told him to stop the mail train. It was on my mind. The next thing I knew, I was in hospital.

In a series of actions that demonstrated incredible courage and presence of mind, four civilian railwaymen had averted a terrible disaster: the explosion of 400 tons of bombs in the middle of a sleeping English country town. Nightall and Bridges – the fireman and the signalman – paid with their lives. In the locomotive Ben Gimbert had attempted to continue towards open country with the burning wagon and its load of forty-four 500lb bombs; he had scarcely cleared the station when more than 5 tons of high explosive went off with an earth-shattering blast, gouging a crater 15 feet deep and more than 60 feet wide.

Gimbert was thrown well clear of the engine by the explosion, landing on grass in front of the Station Hotel. Little was left of the wagon that had contained the bombs. The locomotive was damaged and its tender destroyed. A safe distance behind them, the remaining wagons, containing hundreds of tons of high explosive, remained intact but for minor shrapnel damage.

The fourth railwayman, the train guard, Herbert Clarke, also survived the explosion. He had run almost the length of the train to assist Jim Nightall detach the locomotive and the burning first wagon, and then been thrown 80 feet back by the blast. Recovering, he realised the huge risk of the express mail train colliding with the now immobilised munitions wagons, and had gone more than two miles up the line laying a series of warning detonators to alert the mail train's crew to the danger ahead.

The blast had shattered windows all over Soham and caused widespread structural damage. The gasworks were set on fire. There were casualties, among them the station master and his family, whose house collapsed around them. All survived. Hundreds of other homes in Soham had sustained damage, much of it minor; only thirteen were beyond repair. It took three years to repair the damage.

With Britain fully mobilised for war, help was swift in coming. Local firefighters quickly extinguished the blaze at the gasworks. Emergency services from nearby towns, and from RAF and USAAF bases, dealt with major and minor injuries; local Red Cross volunteers ferried patients to White Lodge Hospital, Newmarket, well into the following afternoon; and shelters were quickly established for those whose homes were uninhabitable. Cooked food arrived from emergency depots and mobile kitchens to sustain emergency workers. Emergency ration cards were issued to ensure that victims of the explosion had access to food and clothing, and a mobile laundry appeared. The response was orderly. The nation had been prepared for much, much worse.

At the scene of the explosion, rescue workers recovered the body of Jim Nightall from the rubble under the locomotive. They found him bare-chested, his skin scalded by escaping steam, and 'his head resting on an arm as if in sleep'.

With D-Day only a few days away, the importance of the Soham line to the war effort – and in particular to the aerial bombardment that would back up the D-Day landings – made its repair a matter of national urgency. At 5.10 a.m. heavy lifting equipment arrived from Cambridge to restore the damaged locomotive to the railway for its removal. Before 11 a.m. bulldozers brought in by troops from US Army engineering units set to work filling in the crater. Soon the well-practised routines of the railway's civil engineering department were at work. Both lines through Soham station opened again for traffic at 8.20 p.m. – only eighteen and a half hours after the explosion the previous night.

Nightall was buried at Littleport, and Bridges – who died of his injuries – was buried at Soham on 7 June 1944. At the subsequent inquest into their deaths the coroner stated: 'They died valiantly in carrying out their duties. They knew the risks they ran and faced them unflinchingly without any thought of themselves, but with primary consideration for the inhabitants of the town. Their courage deserves the highest praise, and to Gimbert, who took his life in his hands, no less tribute is due.'

An inquiry into the cause of the incident, led by an inspector from the Ministry of War Transport, was convened on 16 June. Possible causes considered were the overheating of an axle box in the first wagon, though all axle boxes had been carefully checked at the March depot, and the presence in or on the wagon of inflammable material that might have been ignited by a spark from the engine. No firm conclusions could be drawn. A very serious incident had been contained, and major disaster – one with a death toll most probably running into hundreds – had been averted by the action of four courageous men.

Benjamin Gimbert (1903–76) and James William Nightall (1922–44) – whose award was posthumous –

are the only two railwaymen to have won the George Cross in the same incident. They were again honoured in 1981 when their names were given to two Class 47 diesel locomotives: No. 47577 was named 'Benjamin Gimbert, GC' and No. 47579 was named 'James Nightall, GC'. After these had been withdrawn from service, two EWS Class 66 freight locomotives were similarly named in June 2004, on the sixtieth anniversary of the events of the night of 2 June 1944.

All four railwaymen – Gimbert, Nightall, Bridges and Clarke – have now been commemorated in a memorial, unveiled on 2 June 2007 in Red Lion Square, Soham, just next to the town's war memorial. And people in Soham are grateful to this day to the men of courage who acted as they did that night in June 1944, as expressed by Kathleen Day, who was fifteen when she saw at first hand the devastation caused by the explosion: 'I know that each and every one of us in Soham that night owe our lives to those brave railwaymen, who gave their lives to save our beloved town from oblivion.'

I I

Defeat into Victory

Bill Slim

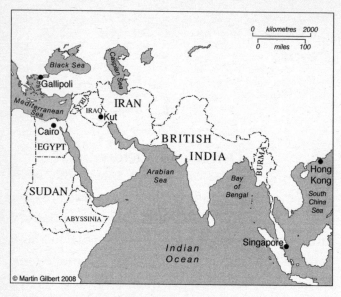

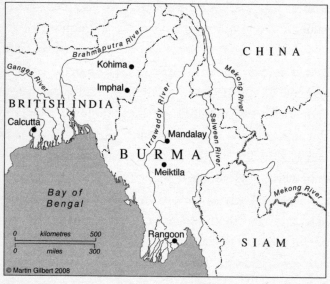

Perhaps the greatest problem facing the senior commanders of Allied forces in the Second World War was that of persuading armies largely composed of citizens conscripted – often reluctantly and doubting – from the democracies to fight and prevail over the very different armies of the Axis military dictatorships: armies that were unencumbered by the democratic values and constraints that we value so highly.

There were various approaches to this problem, such as that of Montgomery, with his strong bond of contact and concern for his men; or of 'blood and guts' Patton ('Americans love to fight . . . Americans love a winner'). But arguably the most successful approach of all was that of a modest, patient, reflective man from Birmingham who largely shunned publicity, who served steadily if unspectacularly in various military commands until 1942, and who then inflicted upon the Japanese Army one of its worst defeats of the war. Bill Slim, an Indian Army officer, was the son of a Black Country iron-monger. In 1944 he led his Fourteenth Army – known as the 'Forgotten Army' – to a famous victory in Burma, went on to serve as a post-war Chief of Imperial General Staff and retired from the British Army in 1955 in the rank of field marshal.

Bill Slim's story is one in which good luck, bad luck and strange apparent misfortunes all played a part. But whatever the twists and turns of his long and ultimately triumphant military career, his personal qualities – modesty, resilience, determination, courage, a capacity for careful analysis, and an abiding concern for the welfare and morale of all whom he led – served him and his country well. As his biographer Ronald Lewin put it: 'Few have surpassed Slim in that gift . . . attributed to Marlborough – "the power of commanding affection while communicating energy". His military distinction was founded on his humanity.'

As a scholarship boy at King Edward's School, Birmingham, before the First World War the young William Slim harboured military ambitions but, for a tradesman's son from the Black Country, Sandhurst was a long way off – both socially and financially. As university was also out of the question for him, he first took a job as an unqualified primary school teacher, then as a clerk in a steelworks. With some Officers' Training Corps experience (which included being demoted for a minor infringement that involved accepting a gift of beer for his squad on a route march) he was commissioned in 1914 and shortly after war broke out joined the 9th Battalion, Warwickshire Regiment, as a second lieutenant in charge of a platoon of sixty men.

Slim's service in the First World War was eventful, though he was never involved in the prolonged trench warfare and mass attacks on the Western front in which tens of thousands of junior infantry officers died. He went with his battalion to Gallipoli, but served less than three weeks there before sustaining, in an attack on a strong Turkish position, chest and shoulder wounds which resulted in his being invalided back to Britain not far from death. Largely through his sheer determination, he recovered sufficiently to be posted abroad again in 1917 with a regular commission as a lieutenant. Again he was wounded, on this occasion in a hotly contested action in Mesopotamia during the recapture of Kut. For his part in this he was awarded the Military Cross in February 1918.

Evacuated to India for another spell in hospital, he recovered, was promoted to the temporary rank of major with the 6th Gurkhas, and took on for the first time the duties of a staff officer at Army HQ. By the time the war ended he had experienced action and injury; he had led men, and looked after them. It was said of him that, however high he rose, 'he never forgot the smell of soldiers' feet'. He had also gained staff experience. That last was important to him: not all fighting soldiers know and understand staff work; Slim did, appreciating it when it worked well, and determined to put it right when it didn't. He knew how much military morale and effectiveness depended on reliable organisation, on the necessities of war – beans, bullets, bombs, and all the rest – and on being in the right place at the right time. Only good staff work could achieve that.

The British Army had increased its numbers hugely during the First World War, and contracted rapidly when the war ended. Many officers who wished to stay on could not do so. Many of those who did endured years of slow promotion. Slim stayed on only by transferring to the Indian Army, reverting to the rank of captain, rejoining the Gurkhas and remaining with them for ten years. Always a serious student of his profession, he attended the Indian Staff College, graduating top of his class, then served in more senior staff appointments before joining the directing staff at the British Army's Staff College at Camberley in 1934. Only in June 1939, when he was forty-seven, did Bill Slim reach the rank of lieutenant-colonel.

By then, with war imminent, the army was once again expanding apace, and once again Slim was despatched to a distant theatre of war. Commanding a mixed and luckless Indian Army brigade against the Italians in southern Sudan in 1940, he made, through over-caution, an indecisive attack on an enemy fort – a lapse that might have ended his command career. However, he escaped such notice and learned a great deal from that, and from a similar operation in Abyssinia, gaining much that would be of considerable value to him later: a clear understanding of the importance of air support, armour–infantry co-operation, reconnaissance, and the dividends that bold action could bring.

More experienced, but wounded yet again – this time during an Italian air attack – Slim returned to India to recover; and once more he resumed staff duties that included preparing for events in the Middle East in which he was soon to be a participant, first as a staff officer then – when a divisional commander fell ill – in command of a division in Iraq in 1941. Action against the Vichy French in Syria followed, then more division-level experience during the Anglo-Soviet occupation of Iran; twice he was Mentioned in Dispatches. Well into his military career, the diligent but self-effacing Slim had been favoured by time and chance, though still only in peripheral campaigns carried out in minor theatres of the war.

But not for long. In Burma invading Japanese forces had begun to drive defending British and Indian Army units back towards the Burma–India border; two friends of Slim from his 6th Gurkhas days, both of whom had become major-generals serving in India, had plans for him. They suggested to their commander, General Sir Harold Alexander, that if Slim were to be put in command of Burma Corps he might be the man to turn things round. The matter was urgent: the Japanese were pressing closer and closer to the Indian border. Alexander, a shrewd judge of character, agreed: Slim was promoted to acting lieutenant-general and flown into Burma, arriving in March 1942.

The situation he faced was dire. All the initiative was with the enemy. Since December the previous year, in a series of swift and daring invasions across a broad front in South-East Asia, the Japanese Army had been invincible. In Burma its units – highly motivated, skilled and hardened in fast-moving, lightly armed jungle warfare characterised by deep penetration and encirclement – appeared to have all the advantages, including those of numbers and air superiority. The territory contested was vast and the terrain daunting – much of it mountainous and jungle-clad, with few roads and railways, all of which were vulnerable – factors that made organised defence by outnumbered, thinly spread and largely road-bound Allied forces difficult, but factors that did not impede the Japanese, who had first entered Burma on 16 December 1941 and were by March 1942 present in great strength, with the invasion of India itself now an achievable strategic goal.

Slim's new command was a scratch team, put together with some desperation to defend a far-off place at a low point in the war. It included various Indian Army regiments – Muslim, Sikh and Hindu – at a time when India's departure from the British Empire was already being discussed. There were also Burmese frontier troops and auxiliary units of varying quality; and some predominantly conscript British armoured and infantry regiments, whose men were not happy, serving in a remote and overlooked campaign a very long way from home. They were also aware of the fate that had already overtaken their counterparts who had surrendered in Hong Kong and Singapore and been taken into harsh captivity. Burma Corps, the nucleus of the later 'Forgotten' Fourteenth Army, was a dispirited, fragmented and polyglot force, already retreating towards the doubtful safety of northeast India, when Slim took it over in the spring of 1942.

Following a series of major reverses morale was low; logistic support – always sketchy – was now crumbling, and in a hostile and malaria-ridden climate, the health of Slim's troops was a major concern to him. But his first tasks were to ensure that a retreat did not turn into a rout, or defeat into disaster. He succeeded in both tasks. In his first months in charge he managed to conduct a textbook fighting retreat, withdrawing his forces in fair order despite an un-helpful higher command – at once both intrusive and unsupportive – back in India. Despite all the problems of handling a large force that was not only with-drawing in the face of seemingly overwhelming op-position, but was itself a disparate entity, he succeeded triumphantly. Withdrawal is never easy, either tacti-cally or in terms of morale; Slim had overcome both these challenges.

How 'Uncle Bill' Slim transformed the unpromising Burma Corps of 1942 into the united, self-confident and victorious Fourteenth Army of 1945 has become military legend. The best account of it is Slim's own, in his book *Defeat into Victory*, published in 1956 to considerable acclaim. As a military memoir it is re-markable because it modestly reflects the man himself: making mistakes and learning from them; studying the enemy and learning from him; acknowledging the harsh realities of combat; and recognising how every soldier's individual motivation can and must be fos-tered and maintained. Slim understood that the duties of leaders included that of communicating clearly and realistically the nature of the challenges faced, as well as that of ensuring all necessary material support to overcome those challenges.

Beginning with the units led by the two officers whose realisation of his qualities had brought him to

Burma, he visited every part of his retreating army. As he recalled in his memoir: 'Whenever I could get away from my headquarters . . . I was in these first few months more like a parliamentary candidate than a general – except that I never made a promise.' A veteran of that time remembers the difference it made: 'He felt that when the times are at their worst, the leaders need to be in the presence of their soldiers. Slim's visits took much time and effort. In some cases language differences posed problems. Slim was not an orator, but understood that all that was necessary was to know what he was talking about and say it from the heart. He spoke from his heart and strengthened theirs.' In Slim's own words:

> What has a soldier got? He has got his country, but that is far away. In battle, the soldier has only his sense of duty, and his sense of shame. These are the things which make men go on fighting even though terror grips their heart. Every soldier, therefore, must be instilled with pride in his unit and in himself, and to do this he must be treated with justice and respect.

For the rest of the war, Slim spent much of his time visiting and speaking to the officers and troops he led, establishing in the least promising of circumstances a bond between leader and led in a force that grew to number more than one million.

Slim's experience and his frankness made for compelling listening. After the great victories at Kohima and Imphal in 1944 he told the officers and men of the 11th Division:

I have commanded every kind of formation from a section upwards to this army, which happens to be the largest single one in the world. I tell you this simply that you shall realise I know what I am talking about. I understand the British soldier because I have been one, and I have learned about the Japanese soldier because I have been beaten by him. I have been kicked by this enemy in the place where it hurts, and all the way from Rangoon to India where I had to dust-off my pants. Now, gentlemen, we are kicking our Japanese neighbours back to Rangoon.

Slim meant it, and his men drove the Japanese back to Rangoon and beyond. But there was far more to Slim's leadership than the innumerable blunt and soldierly speeches he delivered in base camps and jungle clearings, from the back of jeeps and trucks, at remote airstrips, and inside dripping tents. He was a practical, intelligent and extremely knowledgeable professional soldier; he matched his battlefield experience and his staff officer's grasp of logistics to the needs of the troops he knew and understood. In a remarkably short time, he transformed the way Fourteenth Army was looked after, trained, and fought.

As a result of Slim's close attention to the needs and problems facing his men, malaria, once rife, ceased to be a problem. Effective daily preventive medication had always been available, but poor medical support, loose discipline and a widespread suspicion that the pills caused impotence, had allowed sickness rates from a preventable illness to get out of control. An information campaign, backed up by disciplinary sanctions for non-compliance, greatly increased the health of Slim's army and the effectiveness of each of its component units.

Slim was coolly realistic about jungle warfare and its temptations. 'A patrol leader can take his men a mile into the jungle, hide there, and return with any report he fancies . . .' he later wrote. 'Only discipline – not punishment – can stop that sort of thing; the real discipline that a man holds to because it is a refusal to betray his comrades.' Slim therefore set about raising the standards of jungle warfare in Fourteenth Army to match those of the Japanese, and then he improved them further still.

Training was relentless and realistic; tactics were

evolved to counter the standard deep penetration and encirclement methods of the Japanese, who in turn found their positions penetrated and encircled by ever more confident and aggressive Allied units. Reliance on motorised transport fell, as more mobile, lightly armed units using mule transport became the norm. Larger Allied forces – supplied and supported from the air as Allied air superiority grew – established defensive 'boxes' deep inside enemy-held territory that invited attacks that regularly turned into battles of attrition, in which the Japanese lost. The encounters at Kohima and Imphal from April to July 1944 were large-scale and highly successful examples of this method. Such was the change in the mindset of the armies in Burma that to be surrounded had become an opportunity to prevail.

By 1945 Slim was firmly on the offensive. The long march of his Forgotten Army, much of it through trackless jungle, had begun at the Indian border. Without the meticulous planning of transport and supplies to support the hundreds of thousands of troops involved it would have failed; that had been the fate of the long-range Japanese offensive against Slim's forces in 1944. But by 1945 the logistics of Fourteenth Army were every bit as good as its morale and its training. The crossing of the Irrawaddy River was achieved over the longest Bailey bridge of its time, the components of which arrived both by air and by mule. The Allies had at last succeeded in breaking out on to the central Burmese plain.

The battle for the Japanese stronghold of Meiktila began on 4 March 1945 and lasted until 28 March. Mandalay fell on the 21st. Three years and a few months after their first invasion, the Japanese in Burma were in full retreat. Harassed by Operation Character, a vast and well-coordinated offensive conducted by irregular Burmese forces, and beaten in the field by the continuing advance of Slim's army, they fell back on Rangoon. Soon that city too was assailed, and taken by a land assault under Slim, a major amphibious landing, and – just to be sure – an airborne operation.

The Japanese Army's defeat in Burma was final and unequivocal, a disaster without parallel in their land war. Slim's triumph of logistics had been followed by a series of brilliant battles of manoeuvre resulting successively in the fall of Meiktila, Mandalay and Rangoon. These offensives later prompted Admiral Mountbatten, the Supreme Commander at South-East Asia Command, to rank Slim as the best British general of the Second World War. For the same reason, and more recently, the historian Dr Duncan Anderson, head of the Department of War Studies at the Royal Military Academy Sandhurst, put Slim in the same class as the German generals Guderian and Manstein, and the American Patton.

By 6 May 1945 the Burma war was effectively over: a major triumph for the Allies, but one largely overlooked back in Britain, where preparations were now in hand to celebrate the German surrender with VE Day, already fixed for the 8th, a coincidence of timing that was to add substance to the 'forgotten' tag forever attached to Fourteenth Army.

Between Slim's first retreat in Burma and his eventual ejection of the beaten Japanese armies, there had been many setbacks, retreats and even defeats. But Slim's resilience, the transformation he had effected on his army, and the growing trust of all who served under him in the man they called 'Uncle Bill', eventually won through. The modest general who wrote: 'To be cheered by troops whom you have led to victory is grand and exhilarating; to be cheered by the gaunt remnants of those whom you have led only in defeat, withdrawal and disaster, is infinitely moving – and humbling,' himself remained to the end a humble man.

The final word on what Slim achieved in Burma might come best from a veteran of that campaign:

'Bill' Slim was to us a homely sort of general: on his jaw was carved the resolution of an army, in his stern eyes and tight mouth resided all the determination and unremitting courage of a great force.

His manner held much of the bulldog, gruff and to the point, believing in every one of us, and as proud of the 'Forgotten Army' as we were. I believe that its name will descend in history as a badge of honour as great as that of the 'Old Contemptibles'.

Afterword

For some years I have worked on this short book, returning to it when I could, and always with the same feelings: a historian's curiosity about significant events now receding into the past; and a growing reverence, as I learned more and more about them, for the individuals by whom history was being made. So the time I spent reading, thinking and writing about courage in wartime was for me at once humbling and awe-inspiring – all the more so when I reflected on how little of the heroism of that heroic generation a book such as this can describe in detail.

The experience has left me with vivid and enduring impressions of the Second World War; of moments, and indeed months, of its dangers and their many aspects, and with a sense of wonder at the many forms courage took in facing them. And the more I learned the more I came to see the courage of the people whose deeds I describe not just as the highest manifestation of the spirit of the wartime generation now passing from our midst, and as an essential precondition of victory against forces of unimaginable darkness in that great conflict, but also as a living legacy that enriches our nation – and survives and serves us still in a world that is greatly changed.

And there were many ways in which that courage was demonstrated. No single deed marked Richard Stannard out for a VC. His award recognised outstanding leadership, courage, ingenuity and determination in a rearguard action against far more powerful forces. He commanded a requisitioned trawler that was small, slow and only lightly armed, and yet, over four days, and under fierce attack, he defied the odds, repeatedly taking the initiative in rapidly changing circumstances. As a mature professional seafarer and a wartime Naval Reserve officer, he reached and exceeded the highest expectations of the Senior Service. I wrote about Godfrey Place, a younger man and a regular naval officer, because of the imperturbable calm with which he undertook the riskiest mission yet devised for the fledgling X-boat flotilla. He too succeeded against the odds, quietly and resourcefully overcoming the multiple layers of elaborate defences protecting the huge, high-value target he eventually succeeded in putting out of action.

Both Stannard and Place demonstrated, to the highest degree, professional skills and determination in command of vessels among the smallest sent out by the Royal Navy in the Second World War, and there is no doubt that the ethos of that service played a large part in the way they responded to the challenges they faced. As William Golding, later a novelist but in wartime an RNVR officer, wrote of his experiences then: 'I was enormously impressed by the Navy, because it worked. It was full of professional skills; full of people who knew what it was for.' From its battleships and aircraft carriers right down to the tiny X-class submarines, that ethos prevailed; and while it accounts for much of what was achieved by HMS *Arab* and *X-7* in Norwegian waters now nearly seventy years ago, the sheer indomitable courage and resolution of their commanders stands out, and inspires us still today.

Similarly, the story of John Bridge, the supremely disciplined and experienced master of his chosen field of mine and bomb disposal, reflects that ethos of professionalism, and to it adds courage of the highest order. Bridge admitted to being a reluctant combatant, but once he made up his mind that war, while tragic, was unavoidable and had to be fought and won, he did everything in his power to work for victory. Again and again, he faced the lonely challenges of disarming lethal ordnance of types known and unknown, with instant death in prospect as the result of the smallest error. Throughout the war he led his teams, acquired skills that could be acquired in no other way, and taught others to follow in his footsteps. Rightly, the Royal Navy remembers him, and has named its diving head-quarters at Horsea Island, Portsmouth, in recognition of his contribution to the development of clearance diving. In the words on the Commanding Officer of the Fleet Diving Squadron, speaking at the naming ceremony in February 2007: 'He was the founding father of our specialisation, and our new-found know-ledge of his courage and professionalism will inspire future generations of clearance divers.'

Graham Hayes and Geoffrey Appleyard, boyhood friends and happy warriors together in the Small Scale Raiding Force, seem to me to show another side of courage. Their near-piratical adventures in a converted Brixham trawler off the West African coast demon-strated flair and adventure, subterfuge and imagination – surely the key elements of successful irregular warfare. Later, and somewhat insubordinately, Appleyard pressed in a memo for more widespread and aggressive cross-Channel action to prepare for the liberation of Europe. And time and time again he and Hayes under-took raids on the enemy coast, against ever more formidable and well-organised defences, until the grim encounter near Cherbourg that separated them in 1942.

The war in the air also imposed that challenge of going again and again into danger, and never more relentlessly than for the men of Bomber Command;

55,573 – nearly half of its total force – were killed. It is against that background of vast casualties that the conduct of Leslie Manser on the last – and for him fatal – flight of the Manchester bomber L7301 reflects something greater: a steady determination in the face of ever-mounting adversity. Despite equipment failure, enemy action, fire and impending disaster, he successively reached and bombed his target; attempted to take his aircraft and crew home; and then, when all else failed, ordered them to bail out, sacrificing himself to save his crew.

In occupied Europe, where a ruthless totalitarian regime ruled for most of the war, the men and women of whom I have written defied that regime and took risks that scarcely bear imagining today. In contrast to servicemen and -women in uniform, supported in organised units by the forms and comradeship of service life, they operated – some virtually alone – within and against a system of terrible, lawless cruelty. Charles Coward, who calmly pitted his wits against the machinery of mass murder at Auschwitz, and the British prisoners of war who protected the otherwise doomed Sara Matuson, worked to save the lives of others at great and immediate risk to their own. They were under no obligation to do so, and to practise such altruism in such appalling circumstances, as they did, and as Jane Haining did in German-occupied Budapest, is surely impressive: such other-directed courage – illicit, selfless, persistent and effective in the face of brutal tyranny – is truly a triumph of the human spirit.

Those who volunteered for service with the Special Operations Executive faced similar risks, though primarily in the pursuit of essential military objectives: supporting the resistance and preparing for the eventual liberation of Europe. They too accepted terrible odds – it is said that four out of every five died – and they did so because they believed in what they were doing. The two brief SOE careers I have described, those of Joseph Antelme and Violette Szabo, demonstrate a commitment to the ultimate cause of Allied victory and the more immediate goal of the liberation of France – a commitment to which each remained faithful even unto death. Their individual motivation may have differed – Antelme, at first sight an unlikely SOE prospect, seems to have volunteered because he had skills and experience he thought might be useful. Szabo, a young war widow whose Free French soldier husband had died in combat against German forces in North Africa, had more personal feelings to drive her on: those of bereavement and grief. But, as she told friends, life offered chances that could be seized and used to do good for causes you believed in. The ingenuity and persistence of Antelme and Szabo in circumstances of constant danger, the successes they achieved, and their ultimate sacrifice are worth highlighting, not simply for the courage they showed, but to remind us of the courage of the hundreds of their SOE colleagues who, like them, did not return.

The Normandy landings were unprecedented in scale, and in risk too: General Eisenhower, in overall command, had prepared a sombre statement to broadcast in the event of failure. Operation Overlord took a million soldiers, most of them new to combat, from months or even years of training into sudden, violent fighting. The Special Air Service paratroopers whose costly diversionary aerial attack operation did so much to tip the balance on Omaha Beach are little remembered, but they did not die in vain. Today we still rely on the valour of their SAS successors in vital operations, many of which come to public knowledge only years afterwards. And the battlefield courage of Company Sergeant Major Hollis in the first hours following the landing of the 6th Green Howards on Gold Beach remains legendary, not just within his regiment but in the annals of the British Army, as the holder of the only VC of the Normandy landings.

The most striking aspect of the courage shown by brothers Derek and Hugh Seagrim is the contrast between the battlefield valour of the former in North Africa, and the sustained courage his younger brother demonstrated over twenty-six months behind enemy lines in Japanese-occupied Burma. Both were undoubtedly courageous, but in very different ways: the former under heavy fire, leading his men from the front in conditions reminiscent of the trench warfare of 1914–1918; the latter isolated, wounded, out of touch with Allied forces for much of the time, and eventually at constant risk of betrayal, yet still committed to training and organising the irregular units of Karen tribesman who would one day play an important part in the final rout of the enemy and its expulsion from Burma. And while Derek Seagrim's death from wounds weeks before the announcement of his VC is a tragic irony of war, his brother Hugh's attempts in his last days and hours to save the lives of his Karen fighters by sacrificing his own seems to me to reflect both his loyalty to them and his enduring Christian faith.

Though religion undoubtedly played a part in Hugh Seagrim's life and in his approach to his death, the courage of Eric Liddell, uniquely among those I have written about, appears to derive primarily from his deep religious faith. That faith is remembered now mainly because it precluded his participation in his best event in the Paris Olympics; but, when his whole life is taken into account, it shines far more brightly in the way he continued with his missionary work amid the growing dangers of civil war and the Japanese occupation of China, and in the way he organised, led, and provided inspirational pastoral care and support for his fellow internees in the camp at Weihsien. And although in 1945 liberation was tragically denied him by a fatal illness, his memory lives on: rightly honoured by Edinburgh University, his alma mater, and by the Chinese authorities too, with a memorial unveiled only in 1991.

When, after Dunkirk, Britain stood alone against the Axis, and then came under air attack from bomber squadrons based just across the Channel, the civilian population was severely tested but was, to a greater extent, prepared. The home front of a nation organised for total war had defences of its own, and the men and women of the Auxiliary Fire Service played its part in them and took casualties. Hugh Errington was only one of its many heroes: his courage in the London Blitz serves to remind us of the risks civilians ran, and the many who rose to overcome them. And though the dramatic events that resulted in the small town of Soham being saved from devastation were little publicised at the time – all attention was focused on the invasion of northwest Europe which occurred just four days later – the courageous railwaymen involved, particularly Gimbert and Nightall, are surely to be remembered every bit as gratefully as we remember the bravest men who fought in Normandy that same month in 1944.

When William Slim assumed command of the force that was to become the Fourteenth Army, he took on a seemingly impossible task: that of turning disparate and dispirited units retreating towards the Indian border into a force effective enough to take on and defeat the hitherto invincible Japanese Army. That he succeeded is a tribute to his courage, and to much else besides. Slim, who had fought and been wounded as a junior officer in the First World War, and who rose in the Second to lead the Fourteenth Army, Britain's largest single army unit, succeeded in his task because his approach to leadership recognised the vast social change that had occurred between 1918 and 1939, and responded to it with understanding and pragmatism. The 'lions led by donkeys' caricature of the British Army in the First World War had a grain of uncomfortable truth in it. Slim, the ironmonger's son who 'no matter how high he rose never forgot the smell of soldiers' feet', got the best out his men by taking their best interests to heart, in ways that included honest explanation, realistic training, and detailed attention to supplies and medical support. His innovative leadership, well suited to a more democratic era, bestowed on him the power of 'commanding affection while communicating energy'. His men responded: in war by delivering victory, and in peacetime by making their 'Uncle Bill' President of the Burma Star Association, which for decades brought together old comrades from that campaign. It was an honour he cherished for the rest of his long life.

Why then, more than sixty years after that conflict came to an end, and when the numbers of its survivors dwindle by the year, should we remember the courage of the men and women of Britain who fought and eventually prevailed in the Second World War? I believe there are two main reasons: what their stories tell us about courage, and the significance of their legacy today.

Although the origins and nature of the many kinds of courage I have described remain essentially mysterious, the classification proposed by the academic Frank Farley helps a little, if only descriptively. 'Career courage' – that shown by members of the armed services and others, such as firefighters – reflects both a culture and a system of training in which risk and danger, and how to face them, are integral to the role. Clearly wartime courage is largely that, and is seen widely throughout this book, with many variations. Farley's second category, that of 'sustained altruism', features too, in the stories of Jane Haining and Eric Liddell, both of them civilians. And the story of Hugh Seagrim, a career soldier who led the Karen Levies in action, and who for more than two years sacrificed all comforts and risked and eventually offered his life for them too, seems to me to demonstrate both.

Farley's third category, 'situational courage' – that shown by people who simply rise to the occasion –

might cover the undoubted heroism of the men who saved Soham from disaster. Though as railwaymen in wartime they undoubtedly had safety as their highest priority, nothing in their training would have prepared them for the few minutes they had to prevent what would have been the largest explosion yet occurring in Britain. They all risked death, and two of them died; hundreds, if not thousands, were saved from death by their actions.

But to describe categories and then to categorise is simply that, and is not to explain. What I have learned of wartime courage over the time I have worked on this book is simply that it is infinitely more complex than it seems at first. I learned that those who show it come from many different backgrounds, and demonstrate their courage in many different ways; that both civilians and servicemen and -women are capable of it to the highest degree; that the service life, by its ethos and through its training, systematically and successfully fosters and rewards courage; but that the individual manifestations of high courage remain just that – individual, awe-inspiring, difficult to explain or essentially inexplicable. For us today they are a precious component of our national heritage.

Wartime courage, and the sacrifice it so often entails, is something we should continue to recognise and cherish, though much has changed in the last six decades. The huge forces Britain deployed in the Second World War have given way to the smaller and much more highly equipped forces of today; and the brutal simplicities of state-on-state warfare have largely been replaced by the complexities and challenges of making and keeping peace in failing states and broken societies.

So today, as even the Falklands War fades from public memory, we must make it easier for young people to be aware of the role of the courage, comradeship, service and sacrifice that has safeguarded our freedoms down the ages. And we should take pride that these abiding values remain as strong as ever in our armed services, as two examples from Afghanistan readily show. In August 2007 Captain David Hicks of the Royal Anglians, in charge of an outpost under attack by Taliban forces, was wounded but refused evacuation by helicopter, and even treatment with morphine for his pain, in order to command the continued defence of the position. He died later that day. And in February 2008 a young Royal Marine Reserve corporal, Matthew Croucher, threw himself on top of grenade that had been activated by a tripwire while he was out on patrol. He was saved by his backpack and his body armour, but had risked his life to spare his comrades from near-certain injury or death. He was awarded a well-deserved George Cross.

But as the nature of war has changed, far fewer of us have served in the forces or have had close contact with family members who have. So I believe it is now all the more important that we continue to value and remember those who serve and have served, and to recognise in new ways what they have done and still do. Most importantly, as the Royal British Legion has made clear, we must fully recognise what we owe to those who have been wounded in the service of our country, and to their families. Their needs are sometimes great and must be met as they deserve. The military covenant is one of mutual commitment, and the entirety of our society in every generation has a duty to honour it.

I have written about these accounts of wartime courage because I wanted to try to learn more about it, and about the experience of that 'greatest generation' in a conflict that raged around the world. As I worked I came to realise that the courage, sacrifice and eventual triumph of that generation represents not just a noble history but something more: a precious store of moral capital that following generations, inspired by it, can draw on in another age. And if this short book contributes even a little towards that store, I shall be more than happy.

Sources and Select Bibliography

In addition to Public Record Office files, the following sources were consulted:

1. Richard Stannard and Godfrey Place

Independent, 30 December 1994
The Times, 9 February 2006

http://www.bbc.co.uk/ww2peopleswar/stories/77/
a3237077.shtml
Loughton & District Historical Society: http://
theydon.org.uk/lhs/Downloads/LHS%20144.pdf
The Royal Naval Reserve website: http://www.
royal-naval-reserve.co.uk/namsen-fjord/
reports2.htm

2. John Bridge

Personal interview with John Bridge, September 2006

Personal interview with Liz Eastwood (daughter of John Bridge), October 2007

http://www.bbc.co.uk/ww2peopleswar/stories/01/a4270501.shtml

3. Geoffrey Appleyard and Graham Hayes

Appleyard, J. E., *Geoffrey* (London: Blandford Press, 1946)

Six-page typed memoir written by Austen Hayes (brother of Graham Hayes)

4. Leslie Manser

Baveystock, Leslie, *Wavetops at my wingtips: flying with the RAF Bomber and Coastal Commands in World War II* (Shrewsbury: Airlife, 2001)

http://www.vsdh.org/vsdh/manser/index.htm
http://www.raf.mod.uk/bombercommand/thousands.html

5. Charles Coward, British POWs and Jane Haining

Gilbert, Martin, *The Righteous: The Unsung Heroes of the Holocaust* (London: Doubleday, 2002)

Correspondence with Joyce Greenlees (*née* Haining), whose grandfather was a cousin of Jane Haining, January–February 2008

6. Joseph Antelme and Violette Szabo

Binney, Marcus, *Secret War Heroes* (London: Hodder & Stoughton, 2005)

Binney, Marcus, *The Women Who Lived for Danger* (London, Hodder & Stoughton, 2002)

Foot, M.R.D., *SOE in France: An account of the work of the British Special Operations Executive in France 1940–1944* (London: HMSO, 1966)

Marks, Leo, *Between Silk and Cyanide* (London: HarperCollins, 1998)

Miller, Russell, *Behind the Lines: The Oral History of Special Operations in World War II* (London: Secker & Warburg, 2002)

Minney, R. J., *Carve Her Name with Pride* (Bath: Chivers, 1983)

Ottoway, Susan, *Violette Szabo: The Life That I Have* (Barnsley: Leo Cooper, 2002)

Secret Agents: The Behind the Scenes Story of the Special Operations Executive, a four-part series produced by Darlow Smithson Productions for the BBC. First transmitted September 2000 on BBC2.

Violette Szabo Remembered, a documentary by Marcus R. Davidson. See http://www.violette-szabo-museum. co.uk/TAPE/video.htm

Article on Violette Szabo by Dilip Sarkar. See http:// www.dasreich.ca/szabo.html

www.gc-database.co.uk/recipients/SzaboVRE.htm

7. SAS paratroopers and Stanley Hollis

Gilbert, Martin, *D-Day* (New York and Chichester: Wiley, 2004)

Morgan, Mike, *D-Day Hero: CSM Stanley Hollis VC* (Stroud: Sutton, 2004)

Interview with Mike Morgan, September 2007

Interview and correspondence with Pauline Armistead (Hollis's daughter), September 2007

Interview with Professor M.R.D. Foot, 24 April 2008

http://www.army.mod.uk/air/history/321.aspx

8. Derek and Hugh Seagrim

Morrison, Ian, *Grandfather Longlegs: The Life and Gallant Death of Major H. P. Seagrim* (London: Faber & Faber, 1947)

Correspondence with Mrs Ann English, Whissonsett Historical Society, March–April 2008

www.gc-database.co.uk/recipients/SeagrimHP.htm

9. Eric Liddell

Keddie, John W., *Running the Race: Eric Liddell, Olympic Champion and Missionary* (Darlington, Evangelical Press, 2007)

Magnusson, Sally, *The Flying Scotsman* (London: Quartet, 1981)

Thomson, D. P., *Eric Liddell: Athlete and Missionary* (Perthshire: The Research Unit, 1971)

Interview with Dr Margaret Judge (niece of Eric Liddell), June 2008

10. Harry Errington, Ben Gimbert and Jim Nightall

Day, Anthony, *But for such men as these: the heroes of the railway incident at Soham, Cambridgeshire, on 2nd June 1944* (Seaford, East Sussex: S. B. Publications, 1994)

11. Bill Slim

Lewin, Ronald, *Slim: The Standardbearer* (London: Pan, 1976)

Slim, Field Marshal the Viscount, *Defeat into Victory* (London: Cassell & Co., 1956)

Slim, William, *Courage and other broadcasts* (London: Cassell & Co., 1957)

Transcript of a lecture by Robert Lyman to the Open University. See http://www.burmastar.org.uk/lyman.htm – 18 June 2005

Article by Frank Owen, reproduced from a 1945 issue of *Phoenix*, the South East Asia Command magazine. See http://www.burmastar.org.uk/slim.htm

Index

233

INDEX

A NOTE ON THE TYPE

The text of this book is set in Adobe Caslon, named after the English punch-cutter and type founder William Caslon I (1692–1766). Caslon's rather old-fashioned types were modelled on seventeenth-century Dutch designs, but found wide acceptance throughout the English-speaking world for much of the eighteenth century until being replaced by newer types towards the end of the century. Used in 1776 to print the Declaration of Independence, they were revived in the nineteenth century and have been popular ever since, particularly among fine printers. There are several digital versions, of which Carol Twombly's Adobe Caslon is one.